# BECKY'S NEW CAR

BY STEVEN DIETZ

★

★

DRAMATISTS
PLAY SERVICE
INC.

**SPECIAL NOTE**

Anyone receiving permission to produce BECKY'S NEW CAR is required to give credit to the Author as sole and exclusive Author of the Play on the title page of all programs distributed in connection with performances of the Play and in all instances in which the title of the Play appears for purposes of advertising, publicizing or otherwise exploiting the Play and/or a production thereof. The name of the Author must appear on a separate line, in which no other name appears, immediately beneath the title and in size of type equal to 50% of the size of the largest, most prominent letter used for the title of the Play. No person, firm or entity may receive credit larger or more prominent than that accorded the Author. The following acknowledgment must appear on the title page in all programs distributed in connection with performances of the Play:

BECKY'S NEW CAR was commissioned and originally produced by
ACT Theatre in Seattle, Washington, and was part of the
New Works for American Theatre in honor of Benita Staadecker,
Kurt Beattie, Artistic Director; Susan Trapnell, Managing Director.

**SPECIAL NOTE ON SONGS AND RECORDINGS**

For performances of copyrighted songs, arrangements or recordings mentioned in these Plays, the permission of the copyright owner(s) must be obtained. Other songs, arrangements or recordings may be substituted provided permission from the copyright owner(s) of such songs, arrangements or recordings is obtained; or songs, arrangements or recordings in the public domain may be substituted.

*for Kurt Beattie*

BECKY'S NEW CAR received its world premiere at ACT Theatre in Seattle, Washington, on October 23, 2008. It was directed by Kurt Beattie; the set design was by William Bloodgood; the costume design was by Catherine Hunt; the lighting design was by Rick Paulsen; the sound design was by Eric Chappelle; and the production stage manager was Jeffrey K. Hanson. The cast was as follows:

BECKY FOSTER .................................................. Kimberly King
JOE FOSTER ...................................................... Charles Leggett
CHRIS FOSTER ................................................ Benjamin Harris
WALTER FLOOD .............................................. Michael Winters
KENNI FLOOD .............................................. Anna-Lisa Carlson
STEVE ........................................................ R. Hamilton Wright
GINGER ........................................................ Suzanne Bouchard

BECKY'S NEW CAR was commissioned and originally produced by ACT Theatre in Seattle, Washington, and was part of the New Works for American Theatre in honor of Benita Staadecker, Kurt Beattie, Artistic Director; Susan Trapnell, Managing Director.

## CHARACTERS

BECKY (REBECCA) FOSTER — a woman in her late 40s.
JOE FOSTER — Becky's husband, a roofer, late 40s.
CHRIS FOSTER — their son, a psychology student, 26.
WALTER FLOOD — a very wealthy businessman, widowed, 60s.
KENSINGTON (KENNI) FLOOD — Walter's daughter, 23.
STEVE — Becky's co-worker, widowed, 50.
GINGER — a neighbor of Walter's, single, 50s.

## PLACE

An American city very much like Seattle.

## TIME

The present. Summer.

## SETTING

The play will move without transition between four primary locations: Becky's living room, her cubicle at work, her car, and the terrace of Walter Flood's estate.

In point of fact, these are all ONE area, in place onstage at all times. Furthermore, in the case of the cubicle and car, these areas may actually be a part of Becky's living room, which has been redefined by lighting.

Simplify. It is not necessary, nor is it desirable, to fully depict any of the play's locales.

We have two lives — the one we learn with, and the life we live after that.

—*Bernard Malamud*

# BECKY'S NEW CAR

## ACT ONE

*Becky's Living Room. Evening.*

*Lights rise quickly on the empty room, as we hear what might be a vacuum cleaner running offstage. Next we hear things falling and crashing — being grabbed, discarded, hurriedly put away, and then — Becky appears, in slacks and light sweater, somewhat disheveled, wearing one long rubber cleaning glove. With this gloved hand she is holding a toilet plunger upside down, with a new roll of toilet paper skewered on the handle. In her other hand is a Dustbuster, still running. A cleaning rag is draped over her shoulder. And yet, despite this dubious first impression …*

*She is all charm, the perfect (if somewhat ill-prepared) hostess when she greets the audience.*

BECKY. *(To audience.)* Hi. Hello. Wait a second — *(She turns the Dustbuster off.)* There we go. Sorry. Hi! So glad you stopped by. I was just picking up the house a bit — *(She gives the new roll of toilet paper to an audience member.)* Could you put this in the bathroom when you go? Thanks. *(She moves about during the following, putting things in place, readying the house.)* You know how it is: Things ran late at work — so I called Joe, he's great, you'll love him, you'll probably end up liking Joe way more than you like me. Anyway, I told Joe I was still at work and could he pick up the pizza? — But he was stuck at his jobsite longer than planned — he's finishing up this apartment south of here, good money but a real long drive — and because of the rain last night, god that RAIN last night, because of that he had to — wait — *(She finds an empty trash can and hands it to an audience member.)* See that drip right there. Just watch … *(It drips, just a bit — from the grid — near the edge of the stage. To audience member.)* There. See. Could you put this over there for me? Thanks so much. *(She watches as the audience member puts the trash can under the drip.)* Wait. Let's be sure … *(She waits with the audience member until a drip of water falls into the trash can. Smiles.)* Got it. Thanks. Did I mention that my husband is a roofer? Yes. A very good one. Twenty-plus years, but you know what they say — the shoemaker's kids and all that … *(She continues to busy herself in the room.)* I should wake my son so you can meet him — that would be Chris — that would be his crap lying around here everywhere. *(She quickly holds up a piece of newspaper — offers it to an audience member.)* Sports section?

*(As needed.)* (Here you go.) // (I don't blame you.)

*(Back to straightening up.)* Don't get me wrong, I love my son — fruit of my actual loins — but God forbid he emerge from the basement where he lives as the Eternal Freeloader, sleeping off another night of grad-student angst and two-dollar shots. He didn't even do the one thing I asked of him, which was to get the dishwasher loaded — so, there you have it, that's the update: My son was loaded and the dishwasher was not — but, anyway, this is our humble home: *(She shoves a final magazine under the cushion of a chair or couch, strikes a friendly pose, and says:)* Welcome! *(Beat, looks around.)* Fact is: We need a new house. My friend, Rita — beautiful, wonderful woman, passed away last year, her husband Steve still hasn't gotten over it — anyway, Rita had this theory:

When a woman says she needs new shoes, what she really wants is a new job.

When she says she needs a new house, she wants a new husband.

And when she says she wants a new car, she wants a new life. *(A beat. Becky opens a drawer or cupboard and pulls out a very large [and nearly empty] carton of Diet Sprite. She fishes out a can, pops the top, starts to drink — then, seeing an audience member, she stops. To an audience member.)* Oh, I'm sorry. Did you want one? *(If this person says yes, she digs out the final can, saying:)*

*(As needed.)* (Here you go.)

*(Also: if this person says yes, she turns to the person next to this audience member, saying:)* (Sorry. That's all there is. Money's been tight and we let our Costco membership lapse, so … you know.)

*(Becky now … sits, for the first time in the play. Breathes deeply. And drinks her soda.)* I think we'll just stay here in the living room, if that's okay. *(Points.)* The kitchen's that way, if you need something — but promise me you won't look in the backyard. It's a disaster. Used to be a garden. We should just pave it over. Keep our cars back there. Yes, I know that's terrible — but I need to ask you this: Have you ever really been as happy in your garden as you've been on a good day in your car?

All alone. Radio on. Traffic moving, nice and easy.

Heaven.

*(Phone rings. Becky goes to a cluttered desk or table in the middle of the room. When she lifts the phone, lights immediately reveal this area to be — Becky's Cubicle at work. Evening. Into phone, upbeat.)* Thank you for calling Bill Buckley Lexus-Saturn-Nissan-Mitsubishi, Home of the Fifty-Thousand Mile Smile, this is Becky, how may I direct your call? *(Listens.)* Oh, I'm afraid they've gone home for the night. *(Listens.)* Well, yes, good point: if I'm still here doing paperwork why can't the salesmen still be here selling cars, but that's — *(Listens.)* Yes, right, listen — would you mind terribly if I put you on hold for just a second, thanks so much — *(Presses a button on the phone. To audience.)* Sorry. You know how it is. As soon as you start to have a conversation with someone —

*(Phone rings again.)* Excuse me. *(She answers. On phone, faster now.)* Thank you for calling Bill Buckley Lexus-Saturn-Nissan-Mitsubishi, Home of the Fifty-Thousand Mile Smile, this is Becky, how may I — *(Stops, listens.)* You were on hold. Why did you — *no, I did not hang up on you.* I put you on hold. For *less than a minute* — yes, it was really no more than a sure go-ahead and yell if you want —

*(As the caller presumably rants on the other end, Becky sets the phone down, and speaks to the audience.)* Anyway, this is where I work. I'm the title clerk and office manager. I process the new car sales. This place used to be Bill Buckley's main car lot — his Super-Dealership — but now he's got plans to open a Mega-Dealership three hours south of here, and he's been trolling our offices to see if any of us are worthy to make the jump from Super to Mega. *(Re: phone.)* Wait. I think he stopped. *(She picks up the phone. Into phone.)* Yes, I wrote down every word you said and I'll put it right in front of your salesman when he comes in tomorrow. *(Beat.)* No, wait, is tomorrow Wednesday? He's actually off on Wednesdays, so

— *(Holds phone away from her ear once again. Re: Caller.)* Oh, there he goes again! *(Into phone.)* I'M GOING TO PUT YOU ON HOLD FOR JUST ANOTHER SEC. *(She puts the call on hold again. To audience.)* I've been here at Buckley's for nine years. With Chris in school — and the economy in … flux … just *totally fluxed* — with all that, Joe and I need the money. What else would I do? Bag groceries? Be a crossing guard? Go back to school and study what? — massage therapy?! *(Beat.)* Friend of mind from high school called — my age — husband died suddenly, left her with nothing, no insurance, piles of bills — and do you know what she's doing now? Porn. Older Woman stuff. Tasteful. No animals. Just a little leather and lot of makeup. But, you know what she said? I know what you must think of me, Becky … but you reach a certain age and suddenly you're just … *invisible.* I wanted to be *seen. (Pause, more quietly.)* Anyway: This is where I work. *(Looks around.)* Let's go back to the house.

*(Light immediately restore to the Living Room.)* Joe should be home any minute and then we can — *(Stops.)* My Sprite. I left it at work. Just a sec. *(To the Booth.)* I need to go back to work. I left my drink. *(Lights immediately shift to: the Cubicle. Becky grabs her soda. To the booth.)* Thanks. *( — And is about to walk away when she remembers.)* — Ooops. *( — And picks up the phone.)* Still there? Sorry, I had to run home — but now I'm back. *(Beat.)* Are you … are you crying? *(To audience, whispers.)* He's crying. *(Back on phone.)* It's a car … it's just a car … and if you don't get this one, well … I mean, something else always comes along, right? *(Listens.)* You don't think so. *(Pause, quiet and simple.)* I guess I don't think so either. Bye. *(She slowly hangs up the phone. Pause. And then … her upbeat demeanor returns. To audience.)* Found my Sprite!

*(Lights instantly restore to: the Living Room. Calls toward basement.)* CHRIS. ARE YOU DOWN THERE? I NEED YOU. *(To audience.)* He's a good kid. Studying psychology — which might come in handy. I mean, he's twenty-six years old and I just wish he'd meet a nice young woman who is, I don't know, completely the opposite of every girl he's ever dated. Is that too much to ask? *(Chris enters in basic slovenly college garb, pencil in his mouth, carrying a large textbook.)*

CHRIS. Yeah — hey — what's up —

BECKY. Oh, hi, you're here —

CHRIS. — Trying to study down there, you know? —

BECKY. Yes, I'm —
CHRIS. — Got midterms next week — full load — pressure's on, big time —
BECKY. Yes, right —
CHRIS. — But hey — okay — I'm here now, so: Lay it on me.
BECKY. "Lay it on you?"
CHRIS. You needed something?
BECKY. I need you to pick up the pizza. Down at Angelo's. Money in my purse. Dad'll be here soon. I'll make a salad.
CHRIS. I already ate.
BECKY. I told you I was ordering pizza tonight.
CHRIS. Yeah, but on the way home I was walking by Angelo's — and it smelled good —
BECKY. You already ate there?
CHRIS. I was hungry. I was awake.
BECKY. But I got something special tonight — I had a coupon — I ordered the —
CHRIS. *(Finishing her sentence.)* — The Double Ham and Artichoke Supreme.
BECKY. How do you know that?
CHRIS. I saw the guy write it down.
BECKY. You were there when I called?
CHRIS. He was ringing me up. I saw him write your name down.
BECKY. And you couldn't sit there for twenty minutes and —
CHRIS. Not twenty minutes — more like thirty-seven to forty minutes — because it's DEEP DISH —
BECKY. Okay, okay — but you couldn't call me and say, I'm right here at Angelo's, Mom — I'll wait — read the paper — flirt with some spoiled coeds — and then BRING OUR DINNER home with you?!
CHRIS. I NEEDED TO STUDY.
BECKY. WHAT ARE YOU DOING WITH YOUR LIFE? *(Quick beat.)*
CHRIS. Huh?
BECKY. You're a twenty-six-year-old man —
CHRIS. I thought this was about pizza —
BECKY. — And you're still shacked up with your parents —
CHRIS. Oh, can we please not …
BECKY. *(Overlapping.)* — And, hey, we love you to death but when does a psychology student get around to all that stuff about

self-awareness and the unexamined life —

CHRIS. That's Socrates —

BECKY. — Okay, thank you —

CHRIS. — And that's philosophy, not psychology.

BECKY. — But when does a person *look in the mirror,* Chris?

CHRIS. Do you mean when will I self-actualize?

BECKY. Yes, maybe I mean that.

CHRIS. Most experts believe only a few people in history have ever self-actualized —like Plato, Gandhi, Einstein, maybe Bono.

BECKY. Okay — but at what point do you stop and realize that all your friends have grown up and moved on and *here you are without* —

CHRIS. That's perceptual constancy — the ability to recognize that an object or organism has not changed —

BECKY. Yes, that's what —

CHRIS. *(Overlapping.)* — Even though the surrounding stimuli — their physical characteristics, for example, *have* changed.

BECKY. And once someone recognizes this — this failure to *change along with their age and circumstance* —

CHRIS. I don't think the word *failure* is accurate —

BECKY. — At that point don't they — don't you think hey, maybe I better get out there and do something with my life?

CHRIS. *(Interested now.)* Have you been reading Erikson? His seminal work: *Childhood and Society*?

BECKY. Who?

CHRIS. Because what you're talking about is "generativity" — the term Erikson gives to the age at which a person has the impulse to become more productive, to do something worthwhile with their life.

BECKY. Yes! That's exactly what I'm talking about!

CHRIS. And in most cases this happens in middle adulthood — often right around your age, Mom —

BECKY. No, this is not about —

CHRIS. — And so now that we've got our terms identified, let's begin with general inquiry, for example: *Mom, what are you doing with your life? (Quick beat.)*

BECKY. Me? *(Joe enters, saying:)*

JOE. Pizza! *(— And sets the huge pizza down in their midst, as lights instantly shift to the cubicle. Day.)*

BECKY. *(To audience.)* And right then I thought about Mrs. Tipton.

Mrs. Tipton is awaiting delivery on her new car — our top-of-the-line sedan, black, fully-loaded. Steve, my co-worker, had been her salesman. *(Steve enters, quickly. He wears casual business clothes, a blazer and, incongruously, an extremely old and worn pair of hiking boots. Becky is busy with paperwork.)*

STEVE. Have you seen her, yet? Has she come in?

BECKY. Seen who, Steve?

STEVE. She was sitting across from me — I had closed the sale and I was going over some of the extras and customized packages — she wants *everything,* Becky, that woman *wants it all* — and so I slid one of the brochures across the desk to her — are you listening to me?

BECKY. Right here.

STEVE. *(Sits on her desk.)* And I looked down at her hands, these amazing hands, for a woman her age — the fifty side of forty — just priceless hands, and the thing is: Her nails had this black polish on them, this incredible black, this ebony hue from the end of the known world, with a lustre like the '56 Thunderbirds once had, the blackest of blacks, positively *mesmeric* … and as I glanced down at the jet-black inky splendor of that nail polish, I swear to you … I could see my own face in her fingers. Ten Little Steves looking back at me. And Mrs. Tipton said: Is that all there is, Steve? Is there nothing more to be done? And the tone in her voice just broke me in half. I watched the Ten Little Steves just … nod a little.

You wait, Becky, you'll see: She has this beautiful … *pain.* I mean, I have pain, too — this past year, since Rita died. But not like Mrs. Tipton. A man could fall into that pain and never find his way out. *(Beat.)*

BECKY. Thanks, Steve. *(Steve nods.)* I'll need the bill of sale.

STEVE. Oh, sure. *(He hands her some paperwork and leaves.)*

BECKY. *(To audience.)* You see, when Mrs. Tipton arrived last week — *(Becky's desk phone rings. To audience.)* AUGH! I'll get this told, don't worry — *(Into phone.)* Thank you for calling Bill Buckley Lex — *(The Living Room. Same. Joe, on his cell phone, holding the sports page. Chris is texting, busily.)*

JOE. *(Interrupting her.)* Hey, Beck — it's me.

BECKY. Oh, Joe, I'm sorry — we got swamped —

JOE. Yeah, I figured. Did you see the news?

BECKY. — And I still have these quarterly reports to get out, so you and Chris should go ahead and eat.

JOE. Yeah, we did. Chris brought home a pizza.
BECKY. You're having pizza again?
JOE. Don't worry, we made a salad.

| | |
|---|---|
| BECKY. Carrot sticks are not a salad. | CHRIS. *(Imitating his mom.)* Carrot sticks are not a salad. |

JOE. Hey, I was just wondering if you saw the news. Big story on CNN —
BECKY. What is it?
JOE. — The internal combustion engine has been outlawed. All auto sales ended at six P.M. today.
BECKY. Okay —
JOE. Car dealerships nationwide have been shut down. Workers were sent home.
BECKY. — Very funny.
JOE. And since it's now twenty minutes after nine and you're still not home —
BECKY. Joe, please —
JOE. Are you the only one there?
BECKY. Francine is here.
JOE. Francine is the *janitor* — she's supposed to be there —
BECKY. Joe, I know, I'm sorry …
JOE. — I mean, really, it's just a job, Beck. It's just *cars. (Chris has torn a piece of paper from his notebook, scribbled a note on it — and now hands it to Joe.)* Hold on. *(Reads.)* This phenomenon is known as "normative social influence" — the desire to gain approval through situational behavior, despite not believing in the value of what one is doing. *(Pause. Joe sets the paper down. Waits for Becky's response.)* Beck — you there? *(In silence, Becky hangs up the phone. Turns to the audience. The Cubicle.)*
BECKY. Sorry, again. *(Looks down at her work.)* God. The more I do, the further behind I get. *(To an audience member.)* Does that happen to you?

*(As needed.)* (It's terrible, isn't it?) // (Really? Lucky you.)

*(She hands a pile of papers and a stapler to this audience member.)* Can you give me a hand, for a second? I need these collated and stapled. Just like this. Thanks. *(To audience.)* Okay — quick — before we're interrupted: Mrs. Tipton bought her car from Steve. But the model she wanted — customized, loaded with extras — could not be delivered for another three or four weeks. When I told her this, she said: What's it matter, Becky? I've waited this long.

Then she told me her story. *(And now lights slowly begin to feature the distant silhouette of a figure in black: Mrs. Tipton [played by the actress who plays Ginger]. We do not see her face.)*

Her husband was wealthy, well-known, and — like her — well into middle age. One day Mrs. Tipton stepped out of the shower. Her husband looked her up and down, handed her a towel, said, "Time is cruel, honey" — and left her for a swimwear model. There were no kids. No family to speak of. Mrs. Tipton was alone. She sat on the floor of her white-carpeted living room for the next seventeen days. Then she stood up — put on her shoes — went to the grocery store — signed her house over to the checkout girl … and walked away from her life. Cleaned out all her accounts. Kept just enough cash to buy a really good manicure and this one fully loaded black car.

I asked what she planned to do now. "Drive away," she said. "To where?" I asked. She said nothing.

I handed her my card, told her I'd call the minute her car came in. She looked at me with that beautiful pain: "Is that it, Becky? Is that all there is?" *(The silhouette of Mrs. Tipton fades away, as — Walter, nicely dressed, appears behind Becky.)*

WALTER. Good evening —

BECKY. We're closed.

WALTER. Yes, I know, but I wondered if —

BECKY. You'll need to come by tomorrow.

WALTER. — Yes, but you see, this is kind of an emergency, I need to —

BECKY. The dealership closed three hours ago, so if you'd —

WALTER. I won't take up much of your time. I can write you a check, give you a credit card, have my accountant wire the full amount to you — whatever you prefer.

BECKY. The full amount for what?

WALTER. I need to buy some cars. As a gift for my employees. We have our company breakfast at seven A.M. tomorrow morning and we've had a pretty good year, so I want to get them all a little something. But I'm just terrible at gifts. My wife, Sheila, she was so good at it. She had a *knack.* Knew just the perfect thing to buy for people — no matter what the occasion. But ever since she passed, I'm a total wreck. I'm told I should hire a gift consultant, put a sort of Swag Master on my payroll, but I really wouldn't know where to begin —

BECKY. Look, now is not a —

WALTER. So, I had my driver take me to some stores — I had no idea there were so many stores, they're everywhere — and I walked around those stores, not a clue, no idea what to get, and so I told my driver to take me home and right away, there we were, stuck in traffic … and I looked out the window and I said to myself: *cars.* People like *cars.* I'll get them some cars. So, I know it's late, but may I please buy some of your cars? *(Pause.)*

BECKY. How many do you need?

WALTER. Nine. Just nine of them will do.

BECKY. Nine cars …

WALTER. I could arrange payment for them tonight — and maybe you could put the keys in little gift boxes — Sheila always kept a shelf filled with these neat little gift boxes, fitted with ribbons, just perfect — anyway, I thought I'd just hand out these boxes at the company breakfast and shake their hands and be done with it. *(Pause. She stares at him.)*

BECKY. What … um … what kind of cars would you like?

WALTER. Oh, whatever you think. Nine of 'em. *(Becky hands him a brochure.)*

BECKY. Maybe you should look at this — these are the current models.

WALTER. *(Paging through, agitated.)* Oh, see — this is where it gets tricky — maybe just one of each style —

BECKY. And what colors?

WALTER. See what I mean?! This is impossible! God, I miss Sheila.

BECKY. *(Re: the brochure.)* Towards the back, there are color and fabric swatches — interior and exterior. Plus we offer —

WALTER. No, no, no, I can't do this! My driver is waiting. I'm supposed to be at a birthday party for my daughter and I don't have a gift for her either — unless you count my *entire net worth,* which she'll inherit the moment I drop dead from trying to *buy some gifts for all these people!* — So please, I know how this must sound and how foolish I must look, but … can you help me? *(She stares at him. Then: she takes the brochure from Walter's hands, saying:)*

BECKY. *(All business.)* I recommend our all-wheel drive sport coupe. Very popular. My husband … he always wanted one of these.

WALTER. *Oh, did he?*

BECKY. And the thing is: You wouldn't need to pick colors or interiors in advance — the new owners can do that when they come in. Also: I suggest you buy each of your employees the same car — to avoid the appearance of playing favorites.

WALTER. That's very smart. *(She is quickly punching numbers into a calculator, as she talks.)*

BECKY. They could take delivery almost right away. And if you choose the Top Flight package on each car, they can add any extras they might want.

WALTER. Good. Let's do that.

BECKY. Okay — *(The calculator spits out a very long piece of paper — Becky rips it off — and hands it to Walter.)* Your cost for nine cars, taxes, title and fees comes to this number right *here. (Walter looks at the number for a long moment. Then: He looks into Becky's eyes.)*

WALTER. You still wear your ring. I do, too. I thought about leaving it with Sheila — having it buried with her … *(Touching his ring.)* It was my daughter who told me to hold onto it. That it would be a nice reminder. *(Beat.)* I see you've done the same.

BECKY. Pardon?

WALTER. Kept your wedding ring.

BECKY. Well — yes.

WALTER. It's lovely.

BECKY. Thank you — yes, I wear it because, I mean —

WALTER. Was he a good man? Was he kind to you?

BECKY. Yes — he was — *is* — I mean, he still *is.*

WALTER. Oh, I know the feeling —

BECKY. He's still with me — we're still together —

WALTER. Exactly — that's what I tell people, too —

BECKY. No, you —

WALTER. — It's like she's still with me, right by my side, guiding me through my days —

BECKY. Yes, but my husband is still —

WALTER. — And leading me here tonight. Leading me to you. I'm Walter. And you are … *(She says nothing. He lifts one of her business cards from the desk. Reads.)* Rebecca. *(He extends his hand.)* I'm sorry for your loss, Rebecca.

BECKY. You don't understand —

WALTER. I like that name: Rebecca. It has substance. Ballast. I hope you don't let people call you Becky.

BECKY. Well —

WALTER. Becky is the name of a dull housewife in a sad movie about a poor family struggling to hold onto their vanishing hopes

and dreams. In the movies, a Becky always gets the shaft.
BECKY. Walter, I need to tell you about my husband —
WALTER. And I need to tell you more about Sheila — I think that's healthy, to do that kind of sharing — but let's not do that here. Let me pay you for these cars and then maybe we can go somewhere — get a bite to eat.
BECKY. You have a party to attend — your daughter's birthday.
WALTER. And of course you'd remember that! Of course you place family above everything. Sheila was like that, too. You're right, I should go — and I still don't have a gift for my daughter.
BECKY. Does she need a car?
WALTER. She has plenty of cars. Maybe I'll get her a loft downtown. Kids like lofts, don't they?
BECKY. I bet they do.
WALTER. Here is my card — with my accountant's name on back.
BECKY. *(Re: his card.)* Walter Flood — I've seen that name.
WALTER. Maybe on billboards.
BECKY. Do you advertise there?
WALTER. I am the billboards. I own the billboards.
BECKY. Which ones?
WALTER. Pretty much all of them. Go ahead — you can say it: they're an eyesore — visual pollution —
BECKY. Well —
WALTER. — And all of that is true. Believe me, if I could have made *hundreds of millions of dollars* by doing something *good and noble* for the world, I by-God would have done it. But my father handed me this business and said, "Walter, don't screw it up." You play the hand you're dealt.
BECKY. You must have played it well.
WALTER. Who knows. Life is chaos and holidays. Who can say why things turn out the way they do. All I know is that my life has become the story of a handful of people I met by chance and the things we did together. *(Pause. She is staring at him.)*
BECKY. We have these gift keys ... they don't belong to any actual vehicles, but they look real, and people use them when they're giving a car as a gift.
WALTER. I'll need nine of them, please.
BECKY. And some gift boxes.
WALTER. Perfect. *(Pause.)* May I keep your card, Rebecca?
BECKY. Sure.

WALTER. And may I call you? *(Pause. She stares at him, then turns to the audience.)*
BECKY. *(To audience.)* I made a sound that was sort of a cross between "Mm-hmm" and "Hmm-mm" — *(Walter turns and leaves.)* And I thought, *Well, okay, THAT happened — no big deal, except for the fact that I failed to explain to this kind gentleman that my husband is not currently DEAD. (Joe's voice is heard from offstage.)*
JOE'S VOICE. Beck — you still awake? *(Becky turns quickly to the audience member who has been collating/stapling, and says:)*
BECKY. Oh, jeez — hey — how's it going over here?

*(As needed, quickly.)* (That's great. Good job.) // (That's it?! What have you been doing all this time?!) *(She takes these papers to a table in the room and begins to sort them, as lights expand to the Living Room. Night. Joe enters, in sweats and a T-shirt. Barefoot. Ready for bed.)*
JOE. It's eleven-fifteen.
BECKY. I know. I'm sorry.
JOE. *(Re: the papers.)* And you brought work home?
BECKY. *(To the audience member if they did* not *do the collating/stapling.)* (I didn't want to!) *(Back to Joe.)* I told Buckley I'd pull together some info for his new office manager.
JOE. At the Mega-place?
BECKY. Yeah.
JOE. Has that opened?
BECKY. Two weeks.
JOE. And he's paying you overtime for this, right? — For setting up his new office, on top of running your own? *(The answer, of course, is no. Becky sheepishly looks at Joe … who opens his arms.)* Come here. *(And holds her tight.)* Let me tell you how this goes: You take your shoes off, go upstairs, put your nightgown on, put all those mysterious lotions on your face, climb in our bed, arrange your pillows, and crack open that big biography you've been reading for the past two years. That thing always puts you to sleep.
BECKY. I really want to finish it.
JOE. Don't ruin a good thing.
BECKY. Is Chris home?
JOE. Had a date.
BECKY. Oh, no.
JOE. Some girl he met at a party.
BECKY. Is she a student?

JOE. It doesn't matter, Beck —
BECKY. I'm just —
JOE. — And why would you even ask? He's never going to tell us anything about this girl, any girl —
BECKY. You're right. I'm not going to pry —
JOE. Good.
BECKY. *(Can't help it.)* — Did he say where they were going?
JOE. All I remember is: naked skydiving — shark-infested waters. *(Becky punches him, playfully. Joe starts off, as Becky staples a final piece of paper — heading offstage.)* You coming?
BECKY. Right behind you. *(Joe goes. Becky goes to turn off a final light, and as she does so — her cell phone rings. She stares at it. Looks offstage in the direction Joe left. Then she answers the phone. On phone.)* Hello? *(The Terrace of the Flood Estate. Night. Walter — in a shaft of moonlight — is on his cell phone.)*
WALTER. *(On phone.)* Rebecca? *(Beat.)*
BECKY. *(On phone.)* Yes?
WALTER. My daughter tells me there's a rule of some kind, when a man has been given a woman's number — a twenty-four-hour rule. *(Looking at his watch.)* Well, I'm afraid I wasn't able to wait that long. Still … it's a lovely night … and I thought I'd … *(Voice fades. Pause.)*
BECKY. *(Business voice.)* What can I do for you, Mr. Flood?
WALTER. *(Beat, tone changes.)* Oh, I'm sorry. I'm terribly sorry.
BECKY. Pardon me?
WALTER. Just there. In your voice. I've been a fool, haven't I?
BECKY. Why do you —
WALTER. Mistaking your kind and helpful behavior for something more. God, what a fool —
BECKY. Please, it's —
WALTER. — I'm very sorry, Rebecca — I won't trouble you again.
BECKY. — I didn't know what … you were calling about.
WALTER. I see.
BECKY. You have the nine gift boxes —
WALTER. Yes.
BECKY. — And I've memo'd the sales manager to expect payment from your accountant.
WALTER. Thank you.
BECKY. So, I think … that's it. *(Pause.)* Mr. Flood, are you there?
WALTER. *(Simple, no self-pity.)* Things narrow, don't they? As we

age. The things in our life — our life itself, whether we admit or not — it begins to *narrow.* And the unexpected fades away. *(Hearing this, Becky sits down.)* You surprised me, Rebecca. And even if we never speak again: I am in your debt for that. You are that thing in my life that I thought would never come again … that unexpected thing. *(Pause.)* I'll say good night now. And, once again: I'm sorry. *(Walter begins to hang up his phone, as — Becky turns to the audience.)*

BECKY. *(To audience.)* And the word out of my mouth was supposed to be "Good-bye." But something happened —

WALTER. Yes?

BECKY. *(On phone.)* Pardon?

WALTER. You said "Wait."

BECKY. No, I didn't.

WALTER. I was about to hang up —

BECKY. *(To audience.)* Yes, I did. I said "Wait."

WALTER. — And you said —

BECKY. *(On phone.)* I'm sure I didn't say "Wait." I wouldn't say that. I'd say something else.

WALTER. Such as?

BECKY. Such as … *thank you.* For calling. And … for what you've said. I'm very … *(Voice fades. Joe peeks his head in, saying.)*

JOE. *(Whispered.)* Everything okay? *(Startled, Becky turns — nods.)* Is that Buckley? At this hour?! *(Becky just grimaces. Shakes head.)* Unbelievable.

BECKY. It's okay.

JOE. Gimme the phone —

BECKY. Joe, no —

JOE. Does he have any idea how lucky he is to have found someone like you?!

BECKY. Joe —

JOE. You tell him that or I will!

BECKY. *(Covering receiver.)* — I'll tell him, okay?! — Now please, go to bed … *(And Joe heads back to bed.)*

WALTER. It's that hour, you know. That late hour on a summer night when words come out easily. "Too easily" — Sheila used to say. She claimed most of her friends' heartaches and divorces could be traced to things spoken freely and foolishly, on long summer nights. *(Beat.)* And I suppose I've just done the same.

BECKY. Mr. Flood, don't take this wrong —

WALTER. All right.
BECKY. But you really have to stop talking about your deceased wife. You really have to stop that.
WALTER. And you'll do the same.
BECKY. What's that?
WALTER. Your husband. No mention of him. Is that our agreement?
BECKY. But it's *different,* Walter —
WALTER. I will ask nothing of you, Rebecca. Nothing you're unwilling to give. Keep your husband in whatever place, wherever he belongs in your heart. We needn't speak of him again. *(Pause.)* And now perhaps you've already hung up the phone. But if not … I was hoping to see you. Nothing too intimate — just a small gathering of friends. At my home. Sunday night. A pleasant group. I think you'll enjoy them. If you don't enjoy them, I'll send them home and bring in some other people. *(Pause.)* I'll send directions to you at work. Hope you can join us. Good night, Rebecca. *(Becky ends the call. She goes to a chair, cradling a pillow to her chest, and at the instant that she sits down — the Living Room. Dawn — Chris enters, great mood, dressed to go for a run.)*
CHRIS. Hey, Mom — you're up early.
BECKY. *(Surprised.)* Huh?
CHRIS. Terrific morning out there. Crisp — like Dad always says. Now I finally know what he means! Catch you later —
BECKY. Chris, wait! *(Chris stops, turns to her.)* What's going on?
CHRIS. What do you mean?
BECKY. It's *five-thirty A.M.*
CHRIS. And it's *crisp* out there!
BECKY. You don't *run.* You barely walk. So, what's with the —
CHRIS. This girl I'm seeing — she's a runner. It's so weird and awesome.
BECKY. Whoa whoa whoa whoa —
CHRIS. She's really into it — five days a week — except right now she's on crutches, has some ligament damage —
BECKY. So, how is she —
CHRIS. — So for now *I'm* running and she's driving her car alongside me. We have these really good talks.
BECKY. Let's back up: You're exercising and you're having *really* good talks with a girl. How long was I asleep?! *(Joe enters — dressed for work. Pencil behind his ear. Big mug of coffee in his hand.)*
JOE. Look at this: You all got up to see me off to work?

BECKY. Joe —
JOE. That's so nice.
BECKY. Chris was telling me about a girl he's seeing.
JOE. I always liked Candace. What happened to her?
CHRIS. Oh, not again.
JOE. Even your Mom liked Candace.
BECKY. She was a nice girl.
CHRIS. Candace had no inner life! She was all lipstick and spandex and exclamation points!
JOE. *(Whoa.)* Okay —
CHRIS. I don't need that, Dad.
JOE. Sorry I ever brought it —
CHRIS. *(Overlapping.)* — I'm not looking for a *cosmetic* connection here — I don't require a partner who provides mere auditory and visual stimuli —
JOE. You have your iPhone for that.
CHRIS. Exactly! — I am looking — I would hazard to say that ALL OF US are looking to put our *fundamental nature forward,* in hopes of one day *tapping the wellspring of another human soul. (Joe and Becky just stare at him.)*
JOE. So you don't care what she looks like?
CHRIS. Look, Dad: Obviously the process of finding your soul mate can be greatly accelerated if she also happens to be really hot.
JOE. Okay — good to know. *(Joe leaves, giving a smile to Becky, just as — car horn, outside, is heard.)*
CHRIS. That's her. I gotta run.
BECKY. Where's this girl from?
CHRIS. I'll find out today. We're going on a huge run. *(Horn sounds, again.)* Gotta fly. Peace. *(And Chris is gone.)*
BECKY. *(To no one.)* Peace? *(Steve enters, carrying paperwork, looking for Becky at the Cubicle. Day — but she's not there.)*
STEVE. Becky — I've got those invoices. *(Looking around.)* Becky? *(Becky throws on her shoes and hurries to meet Steve.)*

| | |
|---|---|
| BECKY. I'm here, Steve — sorry — I just — | STEVE. Are you just getting here? It's after ten. |

BECKY. No, I was — I needed to —
STEVE. Did you sleep here? You look like you slept here.
BECKY. I didn't sleep here.
STEVE. It's okay. After Rita died, I slept here —
BECKY. Yes, I know.

STEVE. — Couldn't bear it at home. Couldn't bring myself to look at her things — her hiking boots — her socks — her funny winter cap —
BECKY. It was hard, I know.
STEVE. *(Overlapping.)* — And then, when I went upstairs, there was our little hallway — the paint — the pictures on the walls — our bedroom door. *(A beat, we think he's done, then … )* The doorknob — our bed — the quilt — the sheets — the pillowcases … our little "Mister Dibble" —
BECKY. Yes, you told me.
STEVE. — So you know what I did:
BECKY. Yes, I do.
STEVE. I curled up under my desk and fell asleep. Spent three nights like that. Right here in the sales room.
BECKY. Yes, I know.
STEVE. I see her falling, Becky. My mind goes to this place … and I am reliving that moment on that mountain and no matter how many times it happens: *I can't catch her* — my arms won't *reach* — and all I can do is *watch. (Pause.)*
BECKY. *(BIG change of subject.)* Okay, Steve, what have you got there for me?
STEVE. When did you get so cold?
BECKY. I'm sorry?
STEVE. You were always there for me — you and Joe and the others. You were such good friends — always willing to talk me down the mountain —
BECKY. We just wanted to help, Steve.
STEVE. — But then it changed. Like you turned the page in your calendar one day and said: Okay, time's up. Steve should be over it.
BECKY. No, that's not —
STEVE. We gave him X number of months to mourn good ol' Rita, we took him out for beers and listened to him tell the story of her fall for the two hundredth time —
BECKY. *(Trying to make a joke.)* Three hundredth —
STEVE. THAT IS NOT FUNNY. *(Pause.)* You don't know, Becky … you and Joe, you're *set,* you're *locked in,* you'll have each other forever … but some of the rest of us —
BECKY. I know … I'm sorry …
STEVE. *(Overlapping.)* — I want to get past this stuff. I really do. I'm sick of talking about it, and you must be *really* sick of hearing

it — *(Becky's desk phone rings, but — Steve lifts and hangs up the receiver, in one motion, and never stops talking.)* But it's like yesterday: I'm getting a coffee, and this little boy and his mom are in line behind me, and they have this puppy. So, I'm standing there minding my own business, and I hear the mom say to her son: Why don't you go show the puppy to that sad man over there — maybe the puppy will cheer him up! — and I am really trying to ignore this, but now the puppy is sniffing at my boots and the little kid is saying: Hi, Mister, you look sad — do you want to pet my puppy?

And what I THOUGHT — what I didn't SAY, even though I wanted to — what I THOUGHT was:

You bet I do, sonny boy — I want to pet your little puppy — and then I want to take him for a nice walk, a little hike in the mountains with you right by his side — and as we approach the rugged vista which is our destination, I want to let go of his leash for just a *second,* just an *instant,* right when the path beneath his little paws starts to give way — and I want you to watch your puppy's desperate eyes as he tries to grab at that ground — but his little paws touch nothing at all, nothing but *air,* nothing but you and your screams and you might as well *scream your heart out,* sonny boy, because THERE IS NOTHING YOU CAN DO for that puppy of yours who is falling DOWN DOWN DOWN into a dark abyss that will NEVER EVER GIVE HIM BACK. *(Pause.)*

BECKY. At least you only thought it.

STEVE. I only thought I thought it. Turns out I *said* it.

BECKY. Oh my god …

STEVE. It was ugly. The kid cried till he threw up. His mom dumped a Frappuccino on me. *(Steve sits down. Becky is looking at a printout of a driving route.)*

BECKY. You ever driven out to Cedar Cove?

STEVE. You don't drive to Cedar Cove, Becky — you *achieve* Cedar Cove. Or marry into it.

BECKY. Looks like it's an hour to the ferry —

STEVE. Depending on traffic — then forty or fifty minutes on the water — and once you dock, another hour's drive to the far side of the island.

BECKY. People commute from there?

STEVE. People have seaplanes. What's in Cedar Cove?

BECKY. Oh, just something for a client.

STEVE. *(Instantly eager, curious.)* What client? One of my clients?
BECKY. No one you know.
STEVE. Maybe I do. Gimme a hint.
BECKY. So: plans for the weekend? *(He hands her a flier.)*
STEVE. Oh, you bet — here's a flier — you and Joe free on Sunday?
BECKY. We might — I might have some plans.
STEVE. I'm doing a fundraiser for the wilderness co-op at my apartment — we'll have organic juices and trail-friendly gorp —
BECKY. *(Three hundredth time.)* And your slide show.
STEVE. — And of course the slide show of my hikes with Rita, but this one has a couple new photos — never before seen — which really makes it worth watching the *whole thing over from the beginning* —
BECKY. Okay, great — *(A strange cell phone ring, coming from somewhere on Steve.)*
STEVE. — Whoa, that's me, gotta take this, thanks for talking me down the mountain again — see you Sunday! — *(Stops.)* Oh, they need these by five. *(And Steve plops a huge stack of invoices on Becky's desk and is gone, as — the desk phone rings and rings. Becky stares at the invoices … at all the work on her desk … at her ringing phone, then — she looks to the booth, saying:)*
BECKY. Can I go home? *(Light instantly bump to: the Living Room. Evening.)* Thank you. *(And Becky stands in her home … in silence.)* I used to love a quiet house. Nothing but the sound of my own thoughts. Those were the moments when I was most grateful for my life.

I'd sit and remember what a cute little boy Chris was — before he entered this phase called manhood. *(Becky lifts a framed eight-by-ten photo of a smiling Becky and Joe.)* I'd think about Joe and his great big Soviet-style heart: solid and strong and much bigger than it needs to be. Twenty-eight years of marriage … and counting. When my house was quiet, I could see my life for what it was: content. And complete. *(Becky sets the photo down. Then … She seeks out three women from the audience. Ideally, she will say nothing whatsoever to these women — just approach them and politely gesture for them to please join her onstage. [She may need to whisper, "Will you help me for a minute?" to facilitate this.] When Becky has all three women onstage, she begins … )*

Okay — thanks for being here. Since I don't know you, it

should be easy for us to be honest with each other, don't you think? *(She ad-libs off their responses as needed.)* As you know, I've been invited to a dinner party at Walter Flood's house on Sunday. Which is tonight. Now: If you think I should go to this dinner party, please raise your hand.

*(To the raised hands — "yes" votes.)* (Okay — thank you.)

And if you think I'd be a total fool to go to this party, please shake my hand and return to your seat with my great thanks for your honesty. *(Shaking hands of the "no" votes, and sending them away, as needed.)* (Thank you. God knows: You're probably right.)

*[Note: If all three women have voted "yes," the preceding line is not needed. If all three women have voted "no" and left — Becky is welcome to quickly recruit a few MORE women from the audience, perhaps saying, "I need a different kind of honesty," etc.] Becky now turns to the women who remain.)* Okay, ready? We've got work to do.

*(To the booth.)* Some music please? *(Music: something classic [à la Blossom Dearie's "Give Him the Ooh-La-La"], or perhaps something more contemporary [à la Bonnie Raitt's "Wah She Go Do"], as — Becky, with ad-libs, sends the women offstage in various directions to retrieve her dress.* Her shoes. Her makeup and hair items. Her jewelry. To audience.)* Yes, I know this is usually done offstage — for the same reason that women disappear into the powder room — to maintain the mystery. The mystery to me is why we go to all this trouble just so a man can look at us and think to himself: Wow — doesn't a beer sound good? *(During the following, the women quickly help Becky get dressed, coiffed, and made up. They also bring on her coat.)* Sometimes you just want to look nice, feel good about yourself — is that so wrong?

And if that means getting a little gussied up and going out to a party — what's the harm?

And if that means spending a week's salary on a new dress and then travelling for three hours in cars and on ferry boats, all to arrive at the estate of some loopy widower and a roomful of rich strangers who will take one look at you and say "I think you want the trailer park up the road" — well, if that's what it takes, damn it all, I'm gonna do it.

*(To the women.)* You're good at this. Thank you. Do you want to come with me?

*(Ad-libs off them.)* No, better not. Never arrive with someone

* See Special Note on Songs and Recordings on copyright page.

prettier than you. Yes, it's true. *(In only a minute or two: The transformation of Becky is complete. She looks great.)*

JOE'S VOICE. *(From offstage.)* Hey, Beck — are you still here?

BECKY. *(To the women.)* Oh — you gotta go — if he sees you in here — well, I'm not sure he would see you in here — but let's not take any chances — *(She ushers the women offstage.)* Thank you — thanks so much — *(Just before Joe arrives.)*

JOE. Traffic shouldn't be too bad on Sunday except near the stadium. I filled your car with gas, and put a new flashlight — with fresh batteries — in the trunk.

BECKY. *(With a smile.)* I'm not going camping.

JOE. In this city, driving and camping are a lot alike. *(Pause.)* You look … *(She waits, a little nervous.)*

BECKY. … What?

JOE. Like a million bucks. *(Becky gives the audience women [her dressers] a quick and covert thumbs-up.)* So, is he gonna put you up?

BECKY. What?

JOE. Buckley. Three hours to the Mega-Ship for this — what? — this fancy office party —

BECKY. This corporate event —

JOE. Oh, right.

BECKY. — To wine and dine the regional reps — show them the new store — stuff like that.

JOE. Three hours there, couple hours at this event, three hours back — it's gonna be late, Beck.

BECKY. *(With a smile.)* I have a flashlight.

JOE. Take this. *(Joe holds up a key.)* You're gonna be ten minutes from that apartment complex I roofed. I know the owner. He keeps an extra apartment there. Furnished. When I had some late nights down there, he offered it to me — in case I didn't want to make the drive home. It's small, but clean. Single bed, fridge, towels.

BECKY. Joe, I couldn't —

JOE. It's just sitting there, Beck. He's not renting it till the fall. *(Joe holds up the key, again.)* Just take it. In case it's too late to drive home.

BECKY. It won't be.

JOE. All you'd have to do is call me — say you're gonna spend the night and drive back in the morning. Okay?

BECKY. Okay — *(Joe offers the key. She does not take it.)* but I'm coming home tonight.

JOE. You have your phone?

BECKY. *(Points to it.)* Yes.
JOE. Stay in your far left lane near the stadium.
BECKY. Got it. Joe?
JOE. Hmm?
BECKY. Why are you so good to me?
JOE. Oh, Beck … we've had a nice day — let's not ruin it by having a *talk.*
BECKY. I just —
JOE. Because I know where this goes: "Why are you so good to me?" leads to "I hope I'm just as good to you" and that leads to "of course you are" — "you're just *saying* that" — "no, it's *true"* — "why can't you be *honest* with me" — "I *am* being honest with you" — "no, I don't think you *are"* —
BECKY. Joe, please —
JOE. *(Overlapping.)* — And then pretty soon we're fighting about how much we love each other. That's weird.
BECKY. Okay —
JOE. That's a weird thing to do.
BECKY. — You're right. No more talks, I promise. *(Joe gets her a bottle of water.)*
JOE. For the road. It's cold. *(As she takes the bottle, she can't help saying … )*
BECKY. But, if there was someone —
JOE. Oh, jeez.
BECKY. — Someone who was better than me, treated you better than I did — no, let me finish — someone you were attracted to, liked spending time with, anything like that … I hope …
JOE. You hope I'd be honest. Tell you all about it.
BECKY. … I hope you'd lie. Or not *lie,* really … just not *tell me right away.*
JOE. *(Confused/amused.)* Okay …
BECKY. Because maybe it would just play itself out. These infatuations don't last. Maybe in a couple days, couple weeks, you'd be over it — no harm done —
JOE. No contact, no foul —
BECKY. — Right, but if you'd already told me, I'd be *devastated* — just torn up for no reason at all.
JOE. Okay. I'll lie to you. God, I hope I meet someone so I can try this out. *(Joe hands Becky her coat.)*
BECKY. What about you?

JOE. Hmm?
BECKY. If I ever … met someone like that. What would you want me to do?
JOE. Oh, my plan is a lot simpler.
BECKY. How's that?
JOE. Just tell me. Right away. If that happens, I want to know about it.
BECKY. Even if it meant *nothing?*
JOE. Yes, I'd want to know —
BECKY. *Why?*
JOE. — So I could kill the guy. *(He gives her a quick kiss and goes.)* Love you. Drive safe. *(As Becky moves to a chair in the room, which lights will now reveal as — Becky's Car. Evening. Becky speaks to the audience, as she drives. Her mood is edgy.)*
BECKY. This is a bad idea. Just a terrible idea — a Terrible Idea Which I'm Going To Be Late For, unless I make this 5:20 ferry. Can someone tell me why they put these boats so far from the highway — way out by the water?! I'll call him. Easy. I'll call Walter and tell him something came up. Or better yet, I'll tell him that *my husband is ALIVE and we are still married and I am not the type of person who sneaks around behind his back* — but, of course, I AM that person, apparently I am exactly that person: that *sneaking around-and-trying-to-catch-the-5:20-ferry* person. *(She is reaching into her purse.)* Still — I have to call him. Tell him I might be late. Or lost. Or insane. *(Re: purse.)* And can someone tell me why my lipstick is the *first thing I find* when I reach into my purse — *(Pulls out lipstick.) Unless what I'm trying to find in my purse is my lipstick?!* Then it's nowhere to be found. *(Beat.)* Like my phone. *(Rummaging through purse.)* Oh, come on, Becky — find your phone — you know it's in here — Joe handed you your coat, and you grabbed your purse and your keys and … *(Realizes.)* You left your phone at home. *(Becky's cell phone rings in the Living Room. Same — and Joe answers it.)*
JOE. *(On phone.)* You forgot your phone. *(The Terrace. Same. Walter on his phone, dressed for the party.)*
WALTER. *(On phone, confused.)* Hmm?
JOE. After all that, you forgot your phone. *(Becky's Car. Same.)*
BECKY. *(To audience, disbelief.)* I forgot my phone.
WALTER. Who's this?
JOE. Oh, I'm sorry —

WALTER. Rebecca?
JOE. — You're trying to reach Becky?
WALTER. It's Walter.
JOE. Walter?
WALTER. Yes.
JOE. Are you the new guy?
WALTER. Uh, well —
JOE. She's on her way — probably hit traffic.
WALTER. Who's this?
JOE. It's Joe.
WALTER. Joe?
JOE. She left her phone here.
WALTER. Oh, I see — at *work* —
JOE. When she gets there, tell her she left her phone.
WALTER. I'll do that.
JOE. And tell her to spend the n*ight.*
WALTER. *Pardon me?*
BECKY. In my car …
JOE. She deserves that, right? —
WALTER. Yes, I suppose so …
JOE. — The money they make on those cars.
BECKY. Alone …
WALTER. Oh, they loved them.
JOE. What's that?
WALTER. They all loved their cars. *(Music, under.)*
BECKY. Radio on …
JOE. I bet they did …
WALTER. Thanks for your help.
BECKY. Traffic moving, nice and easy …
WALTER. See you, Joe.
JOE. See you, Walter.
BECKY. Heaven help me. *(Music rises, as — the lights rush to black.)*

**End of Act One**

## ACT TWO

*The Terrace. Night.*

*Cocktail music from offstage, as the dinner party is in full swing. Kenni and Ginger are looking at the view. They each have a drink. They both look smashing.*

KENNI. He bought me a loft.
GINGER. For your birthday?
KENNI. Yes. Downtown. Terrific view. Cost a fortune.
GINGER. Your father loves you, Kenni.
KENNI. *(Beat.)* Do you need a loft?
GINGER. You don't want it?
KENNI. He bought me one last year, too.
GINGER. It's been hard on him. Since your mom died.
KENNI. Turns out Mom was right about everything. She told me exactly how Dad was going to behave when she was gone: said he'd get a little daft about things. Lose his confidence — be a little adrift with people —
GINGER. Sheila was always very perceptive.
KENNI. — And that he'd probably get snookered by a woman.
GINGER. She said that?
KENNI. She knew her friends, Ginger. She knew that once she died, they'd smell blood in the water. *(They both drink.)*
GINGER. Did she mention any names?
KENNI. Oh, come on, Ginger! — Mom knew you'd swoop right in with your charming smile and your backless dress. It's no big deal. Dad's a big boy. Given certain *very clear* boundaries, he can take care of himself.
GINGER. Kenni, I assure you —
KENNI. I sort of envy him. And you.
GINGER. Why?
KENNI. There's no pressure to "find someone" — not at your age.
GINGER. Thanks for that.

KENNI. Or to find the *right* someone — I mean, did you ever meet someone who was sweet and kind and funny and odd and had almost nothing in common with you? — Who had no idea you were from a wealthy family — Someone who just liked you because of *who you were* — and when you're with him you have dopey songs that you can't get out of your head — and all the hard things seem so easy and all the easy things seem so important — I mean, really, Ginger, *it can't just be me, right?* This must have happened to lots of people — this must have happened to you. *(Kenni is staring at Ginger.)*
GINGER. *(Simple.)* No. You're the first. *(Walter arrives, tense. He holds a martini.)* When are we eating, Walter?
WALTER. I wish I knew. I kept following the caterer around the house, asking him about dinner — but he never answered. Turned out he was the exterminator. Why must everyone wear *white?*
KENNI. I'll handle it. *(With a look at Ginger.)* Have fun. *(A charged, awkward moment.)*
GINGER. Walter.
WALTER. Ginger. *(They are looking at the water.)*
GINGER. Lovely.
WALTER. Yes.
GINGER. Your daughter thinks I'm swooping in.
WALTER. Pardon?
GINGER. On you. She thinks I have some plan to swoop in.
WALTER. Well, you know Kenni, she's very protective —
GINGER. Yes, of course —
WALTER. — But I personally don't feel … swooped in … upon.
GINGER. Good. *(They drink. Look at the view.)*
WALTER. I don't see your boat. I don't see either of your boats.
GINGER. The boats are gone. The artwork is gone. The horses.
WALTER. Even the horses?
GINGER. No way to keep them. Or the place at the lake. Or the season tickets.
WALTER. *You gave up your season tickets?*
GINGER. Along with three cars and most of my jewelry.
WALTER. I had no idea.
GINGER. It finally caught up with us — the Timber Baron's kids. We all assumed that the money none of us made would never run out — then the investments went bad, the trust funds got emptied, and the bills came due.
WALTER. I'm so sorry —

GINGER. No — please — the last thing we deserve is sympathy. The fact is: After a hundred years of being pampered and deferred to, *none of us know how to do a fucking thing.* We've never worked. Never had jobs. We have no tangible skills. Oh, sure, we know how to stay *busy* — we're all the time telling each other how *busy* we are — but if we had to walk out the door tomorrow and do something practical, something *useful* — something other than dressing up, attending a function and eating with the proper fork: We wouldn't have a clue.
WALTER. Ginger —
GINGER. If our great-grandpa — the Timber Baron — came back and saw what *soft little spoiled ninnies* we've become, he'd kick our ass to hell and back. And here I am: the woman who kept putting off getting married — putting it off till the last minute and beyond — and I could do that, you see, because I always had this safety net. I had my *money.* And I knew that even when my looks were long gone, I'd still have my inheritance … and maybe there'd be someone who would want *that* … some man who would want my money even if he didn't really want *me. (Kenni appears.)*
KENNI. I found the chef. Dinner's being served.
GINGER. Wonderful. I'm starved. *(Ginger goes.)*
WALTER. I had no idea about Ginger. What she's going through.
KENNI. Mom would say —
WALTER. *(Sharper than he intends.)* I don't want to hear what your mother would say. Not tonight. So … how's the loft?
KENNI. It's nice.
WALTER. Do you paint there?
KENNI. Paint?
WALTER. Isn't that what people do in lofts? That's what they do in the movies. They paint and play the saxophone. Do you need a saxophone?
KENNI. Dad, listen —
WALTER. Or maybe a treadmill? I know how you and Ramsey love to go running.
KENNI. Yes, well —
WALTER. Is he in town?
KENNI. No, the trust fund playboy Ramsey McCord is still back East. Trolling for debutantes.
WALTER. You talk that way — but everyone assumes you'll marry him, anyway.
KENNI. Including you?

WALTER. No — I hope you'll surprise me. I've come to believe in surprises. *(Becky appears, behind Walter. Becky still wears her coat, and still carries the water bottle that Joe gave her.)*
KENNI. *(To Becky.)* Catering staff?
BECKY. Umm …
KENNI. I can show you to the kitchen — *(Walter turns to see her.)*
WALTER. You made it!
BECKY. I guess so.
WALTER. Rebecca, this is Kensington Hermione Flood — my daughter.
KENNI. Kenni. *(Re: catering remark.)* Sorry, I thought —
BECKY. That's quite the name.
KENNI. My mother was a terrible Anglophile.
BECKY. Yes, I've heard a lot about your mom —
WALTER. — But you won't hear another word about her tonight. *(Re: water bottle.)* Now, let's get you a proper drink —
BECKY. I'm fine.
WALTER. Well, I'll get you a tumbler and some ice —
BECKY. No thanks — this is all I need. Really. *(Becky continues to clutch her water bottle like a security blanket.)*
KENNI. Well …
WALTER. Kenni lives downtown. She has a new loft.
BECKY. Oh, right — Happy birthday!
KENNI. *(Odd.)* Thanks.
WALTER. *(To Becky, concerned.)* Were my directions wrong?
BECKY. No — they were fine — but no sooner had I driven off the ferry, but I ran into a breakdown — middle of the road — it was pretty bad — and I didn't have my cell phone —
WALTER. Yes, I know.
BECKY. *(Overlapping.)* — And I was running late — but somehow I made it through and I got here and *what do you mean you know?*
WALTER. I spoke to Joe. *(Beat.)*
BECKY. Really?
WALTER. He answered — told me you'd left, that you were on your way here —
BECKY. He did?
WALTER. Such a pleasant guy. Is he one of the salesmen? *(Kenni breaks in, with purpose.)*
KENNI. Maybe I should take your coat … if you're staying?
WALTER. She's staying. *(Kenni helps Becky out of her coat.)*

KENNI. Okay. *(To Walter.)* We're waiting. *(Kenni goes.)*
WALTER. You look …
BECKY. Like I've been driving all day?
WALTER. … Stunning. Completely stunning. *(As Walter takes a sip of his martini — Becky gives another quick, covert thumbs-up to her dressers.)* I was starting to think I'd made you up. Or known you in some other time or place. Do you ever do that — imagine a kind of parallel life?
BECKY. Umm … *(Walter holds up his martini glass — making a toast.)*
WALTER. Cheers. *(Becky clinks her water bottle against his glass.)*
BECKY. Clink. *(Lights isolate Becky.)* And we went inside. And I was seated across from Walter — with a Nobel economist on my left, and a woman who looked like Lauren Hutton on my right. The food was terrific. The conversation stimulating. And I started feeling braver by the minute. Yes, I'd told one outright lie to my husband and I wasn't proud of that — but no one was hurt. Not yet. And if it stopped here — if I had dinner, said good night and drove home — that would be the end of it. No harm done. *(The Living Room. Joe and Chris — sharing a bag of chips — follow a distraught Steve into the room.)*
JOE. Really? Not one person came?
STEVE. I put up fliers, sent emails to everyone — *nothing.*
JOE. Sorry to hear it, Steve.
STEVE. I had fair-trade coffee in biodegradable mugs!
CHRIS. Doing good is hard, man.
JOE. Have a chip. *(Steve reaches into the bag of chips, saying:)*
STEVE. These are terrible for you. *(And then devours the chip. Suddenly he begins to avidly untie and retie the laces on his weathered hiking boots.)*
CHRIS. You know, Steve, I think this has produced in you a certain level of *dysphoria.*
STEVE. *Dysphoria?*
CHRIS. Think of it as the opposite of *euphoria.* A sort of *stew* of anxiety, restlessness and depression — but you can't really diagnose or treat it like a standard disorder. It's more a state of being.
STEVE. *A way of life.*
CHRIS. Exactly.
STEVE. Can I have another chip? *(Steve takes the entire bag.)* Where's Becky?
JOE. You know — that big shindig that Buckley is throwing.

STEVE. What shindig?
JOE. That corporate event — the sneak peek for the all the industry insiders, down south at the new Mega-'Ship.
STEVE. That's impossible.
JOE. Huh?
STEVE. It's not open, yet. That dealership —
JOE. This is a preview, a kick-off —
CHRIS. She got all dressed up.
JOE. *(Beat.)* You really don't know about this?
STEVE. No. *(Beat.)* I wonder what else I don't know about.
CHRIS. Don't go there, Steve. *(Lights isolate Becky.)*
BECKY. *(To audience.)* Dessert was to die for. And the Lauren Hutton lookalike turned out to be an activist who had infiltrated the dinner to convince Walter to tear down his billboards. She cornered him over the pistachio flan. He took her card. She took his arm. I watched them from across the room and I felt something rise up from a much younger part of my heart. I believe it's called *jealousy. (The Terrace. Later. Ginger enters, wine in hand.)*
GINGER. *(Re: Becky's water bottle.)* Must be some special elixir in that bottle. You can't seem to let go of it.
BECKY. I guess I can't.
GINGER. Well, it's working. Walter seems very fond of you. They all do. *(A beat. They sip their drinks.)* Where's your husband tonight?
BECKY. He's — he — well, he — *passed.*
GINGER. Passed on the invitation?
BECKY. Yes — well — no — away. He — passed — *away.*
GINGER. Really? *(Becky nods.)* How convenient. *(Walter enters, drink in hand.)*
WALTER. Ginger, have you met Rebecca?
GINGER. Yes, I have — and how refreshing to meet someone who actually *works for a living.*
WALTER. *(Lightly, to Becky.)* You'll have to forgive Ginger: She and I have always managed to say to each other exactly what's on our mind.
BECKY I see. GINGER. Is that true, Walter?
WALTER. Well, I certainly think we —
GINGER. Because if that's true, I'd like to tell you this: Sheila was not well-liked. You loved her to death, I know, and she was a good mother to Kenni — but most people found her … *fakey.* Always upbeat, always on the ball, always the right thing to say, the right note

in the mail, the right hand towels for all the right occasions — IT WAS TOO MUCH, Walter, and after a while nobody was buying it.

WALTER. Now, listen to me —

GINGER. That woman was about *as deep as a cookie sheet.* In fact, we started calling her that behind her back: Cookie Sheet — sweet and shallow and completely nonstick. *(Kenni enters.)*

KENNI. They're bringing the cars around.

GINGER. *(Re: Becky, with a smile.)* Be careful, Walter. This one's for real. *(Ginger leaves.)*

WALTER. Kenni, are you staying over?

KENNI. No — I have my morning run.

WALTER. And the cottages — are they full?

KENNI. I think Cottage Four is available. Why? *(Walter says nothing.)* Well … *(To Becky.)* Nice to meet you. Safe travels. *(And Kenni is gone. Becky is looking at the view.)*

BECKY. Lovely. *(Walter is looking at her.)*

WALTER. Yes.

BECKY. This place … how long have you had it?

WALTER. Oh, it's belonged to my family for years.

BECKY. And who did you buy from?

WALTER. You mean the original owners?

BECKY. Yes.

WALTER. I believe the original owners were a sovereign Indian nation. *(Becky smiles. Pause.)* Rebecca, I wonder if you'd —

BECKY. I couldn't possibly stay. If that's what you're thinking. If that's what you were going to ask me. Is that what you were thinking and were going to ask me?

WALTER. Not anymore.

BECKY. According to the schedule, if I leave now I can still make the last ferry —

WALTER. But you'll miss the sunrise over the water tomorrow. Like nothing you've ever seen. Like the first morning of the world. *(Becky again looks at the view.)* You're tempted … *(She looks back at Walter.)* But you're going to leave.

BECKY. Yes. *(She drinks the last drop of her water.)*

WALTER. Let me propose something. Come next week. Take one of the cottages. See me as much or as little as you'd like. But, just … spend a little time here.

BECKY. That's impossible.

WALTER. You can't get away from work?

BECKY. Well, no — I can't, actually — but Walter, listen: the breakdown that happened on the road tonight had nothing to do with cars: It was *my* breakdown. I had a head-on emotional crash — pounding the dashboard with my fists and crying my eyes out and saying, *"What the hell am I doing?"*
WALTER. *I do that all the time!*
BECKY. *(Re: her water bottle.)* Like this! — WHY AM I STILL HOLDING THIS?
WALTER. I have no idea.
BECKY. MY HUSBAND GAVE THIS TO ME.
WALTER. And you *saved it?*
BECKY. YES, I —
WALTER. I DON'T BLAME YOU! Oh, how we hold onto things! Do you know I have a POPSICLE in my freezer — one half of a GRAPE POPSICLE that I shared with Sheila before she died?! *Why can't I get rid of that?!*
BECKY. I really don't —
WALTER. *Let's throw our rings in the water!*
BECKY. What? No! *(Walter is struggling to remove his wedding band.)*
WALTER. C'mon — we'll do it together — free ourselves from the past —
BECKY. Walter — wait — you don't need to —
WALTER. Do it, Rebecca — or let me do it —*shall I do it for you?! (Walter reaches for her hand, but Becky pulls it away — and begins taking off her own wedding ring.)* Let's SAY GOOD-BYE TO THESE BANDS THAT BIND US! — That's it, slide it right off — GOOD-BYE TO THESE SHACKLES OF REMEMBRANCE!
BECKY. My god, you're serious —
WALTER. *Now, Rebecca — do it with me — on the count of three:*
BECKY. But, Walter —
WALTER. ONE! TWO! THREE!!! *(And Walter hurls his wedding ring into the distance, into the water. Becky pretends to do the same — although, in truth, she has palmed her ring in her other hand. Walter does not know this. Silence … as they both stare at the water.)* I don't feel like I thought I'd feel. I thought I'd feel free. But I just feel like I threw my ring in the water. *(He looks down at her ringless hand.)* What about you? … how does it feel? *(Becky looks down at her hand, then up at Walter. She kisses him on the cheek.)*
BECKY. Good night, Walter. *(Walter goes, as lights reveal the Living Room. Day. To audience.)* My house is quiet again. Buckley called

the morning after I first went to Walter's. He wanted to transfer me to the Mega-Dealership — along with a promotion and a raise. Apparently, I sold more cars in one night than some of his salesmen had sold all quarter.

I hesitated. Told him I didn't think I could manage the travel. Needed to talk to Joe. Buckley told me he was willing to sweeten the deal. He ordered me to say nothing about this to my co-workers. And then he offered me an immediate three weeks paid vacation, PLUS a major bonus in the form of a top-of-the-line new car. Final offer. I didn't tell my co-workers. I also did not tell Joe. *(Joe enters. Wearing reading glasses; doing the month's bills.)*

JOE. It has to be your call — like when I did that roofing job down south —

BECKY. Joe —

JOE. — It's a long drive, but if the money's good —

BECKY. What would you do? — with me on the road that much?

JOE. I don't want you on the road that much. Six hours a day in your car — that makes no sense —

BECKY. Right, so why should —

JOE. — So if you really want to take this job, we should think about making a move down there —

BECKY. We can't move down there.

JOE. Why not? People have roofs down there.

BECKY. But all your contacts are here — your clients, your crew —

JOE. I'm just saying —

BECKY. And what do we tell Chris?

JOE. We tell him he *won.* We're moving out before he is.

BECKY. What if I stayed down there? *(Off his look.)* At that apartment — the rental unit you told me about. I'll just use it when I need it. Maybe a few nights a week. And then I'm home every weekend. *(Beat.)* You hate this.

JOE. No, I just —

BECKY. It was your idea — me staying down at that place —

JOE. Yes, right, but —

BECKY. But what? *(He looks at her. Reaches into his pocket. Holds up the key.)* Are you sure?

JOE. Hell, Beck: I'll probably see you more than I do now. *(She takes the key from him, as a light rises on Walter.)*

WALTER. I think about you. For no reason at all *I find myself thinking about you* —how many ice cubes you like in your water …

the way you turn the pages of your books. *(Becky walks to Walter and they embrace; they kiss. The Terrace. Morning. Walter and Becky sip their coffees.)*
BECKY. *(To the audience.)* How does it happen? In only a few days, Walter and I had rituals. Coffee on the veranda; watching the sunset from the dock. I had a hook for my jacket and a place for my keys, and in no time at all … I began to feel at home. One day at the Cedar Cove Market, the cashier said to me: "Are you the new Mrs. Flood?" I smiled … but said nothing. Because it was Friday … *(She puts her wedding ring back on.)* And I was needed at my other life. *(The Living Room. Morning. Chris — having just returned from his morning run — is waving offstage.)*
CHRIS. *(Calling offstage.)* See you tomorrow! *(Car horn honks, in response. Chris bounds in, getting something from the fridge.)* Beautiful morning.
BECKY. Crisp?
CHRIS. Not crisp exactly. I'd say: *pert.*
BECKY. The morning is "pert?"
CHRIS. Sassy. Brazen. Fresh as can be.
BECKY. You're in a good mood.
CHRIS. Endorphins, Mom. Best drug on earth. Home-grown, street-legal, and free of charge.
BECKY. Did you go out last night?
CHRIS. We don't go out — we just *run.* And oh, man, we had a great run this morning. She's almost off the crutches.
BECKY. And what about her inner life — how's that going?
CHRIS. Her inner life is *kicking my ass!* It's amazing.
BECKY. When do I get to meet this girl?
CHRIS. Mom, I don't want to screw this up. *(Points.)* Dad left you a note. He's already gone — two appraisals and an inspection —
BECKY. He works so hard, Chris.
CHRIS. — And, hey, Steve's been trying to reach you. Says you never answer your phone down at the Mega-'Ship.
BECKY. What did he —
CHRIS. I told him to try your cell. *(Becky's cell phone rings, as — )* Gotta shower. *Peace! (Chris leaves the room.)*
BECKY. *(Calling after him.)* Would you stop saying that! *(Becky answers her phone, as lights feature — the Cubicle. Steve is there, calling from her desk phone. Full of confidence. On phone.)* This is Becky.

STEVE. *(On phone.)* And this is the New Steve, calling from your old desk. Do you miss it?
BECKY. *(Lightly.)* I have a desk at my new job.
STEVE. And the Old Steve would have believed that!
BECKY. *(Trying to laugh.)* What are you talking about?
STEVE. It's all a *ruse,* Becky! Did you really think no one would *find* you *out?* There was no big corporate shindig — you're not working down at the Mega-'Ship every day.
BECKY. Steve —
STEVE. They're way behind schedule — nobody's even in the office, yet — certainly not you!
BECKY. Look — I can explain —
STEVE. So this made me think: Why is it that Becky Foster can get promoted to a job *she doesn't have to show up for,* and Steve Singletary — Regional Sales Leader and five-time Customer Satisfaction All-Star — gets left with nothing but a bucketful of snot?!
BECKY. Wait — Steve — listen to me —
STEVE. And so I marched into Buckley's office and spit that question right into his face! And you know what he did? He closed the door, grabbed my arm, and whispered these words to me: *What Becky Foster's been doing for the past few weeks is no one's business but HERS — and MINE.*
BECKY. Oh, god …
STEVE. He's a married man, Becky! And, okay, I'll keep your secret — *even though I don't know how you could do a thing like this to Joe* — but the point is: The New Steve is not gonna back down from the Buckleys of the world anymore!
BECKY. Oh, god …
STEVE. If he doesn't want his wife to know about this affair — it's gonna cost him!
BECKY. Oh, my god …
STEVE. *(Looking offstage.)* Hey — he's here! — he's walking through the door! —
BECKY. Steve — NO —
STEVE. *(Calling offstage.)* MR. BUCKLEY — DO YOU HAVE A MINUTE?
BECKY. Don't do it, Steve! — *(Doorbell rings. Becky ignores it.)*
STEVE. *(Into phone.)* I'm gonna kick it, Becky —
BECKY. — Don't say *anything to Buckley* till I get there!

STEVE. — Gonna kick this DYSPHORIA once and for all!
BECKY. THIS WHAT? *(Steve hangs up, as — doorbell rings, repeatedly. The Living Room. Same. Becky looks at the door — looks at her watch — looks quickly to the audience, saying — )* I need to change. I mean: *everything.* I mean: *completely. (Becky rushes off-stage, calling:)* CHRIS — CAN YOU GET THAT? *(Just as Chris — hair wet, wearing only sweatpants and a towel around his neck — answers the door. It is Kenni. In sportswear, looking great. She holds a pair of crutches.)*
KENNI. It's a lie, okay?! There is nothing wrong with my ankle. I don't have any ligament damage. I just really *hate* running, okay?! *(Throws crutches to floor.)* I hate running, I hate exercise, I hate to sweat, but I really really really like you. *(And she plants a good long kiss on Chris' lips.)*
CHRIS. *(Stunned, happy.)* Thanks.
KENNI. And I have a boyfriend. His name is Ramsey McCord. He's in Nantucket for the summer. Or maybe Barbados. It depends on the winds. I can't stand him. I don't ever want to see him again.
CHRIS. One of the McCords?
KENNI. Yes.
CHRIS. The billionaire hedge-fund McCords?
KENNI. Yes. We grew up together. Got thrown together by our families. But the thing is —
CHRIS. I can't believe you know the McCords.
KENNI. — Right, who cares, it's no big deal —
CHRIS. I read that one Christmas they gave each kid their own island.
KENNI. — WOULD YOU PLEASE JUST LET ME SAY THIS? *(A breath.)* Ramsey is gone. And you're *here* — you are kind and funny and sweet and odd — but the main thing is: You're real. You're real and you are *right here* —
CHRIS. That's called proximate urgency.
KENNI. — *Yes* — sure — whatever —
CHRIS. And that means —
KENNI. — That means you should put your clothes on so I can take you home and rip 'em off you —
CHRIS. Um, okay —
KENNI. — We can take my car — it's parked on the lawn, I never even turned it off — *(Chris is hurriedly throwing on a sweatshirt and some flip-flops.)*

BECKY'S VOICE. *(From offstage.)* CHRIS? —
KENNI. Is that your Mom? *(And now Chris is pulling Kenni toward the door — )*
CHRIS. Let's go —
BECKY'S VOICE. — WHO WAS AT THE DOOR?
KENNI. How great! — I'd love to meet her.
CHRIS. — *Not while your motor is running* —
BECKY'S VOICE. CHRIS? — CHRIS. — C'MON — *(And they are gone, just as — Becky rushes back in — wearing business garb — brushing her hair.)*
BECKY. — Did I hear someone? *(She sees the crutches. Lifts and looks at them, confused, as — Joe enters from another direction, in work clothes.)*
JOE. *(Re: the crutches.)* Hard week at the Mega-'Ship?
BECKY. No — these are —I don't know what these are.
JOE. Forgot my billing folder — *(He gives her a quick kiss, as — she gathers up her purse and keys.)*
BECKY. Oh — okay —
JOE. And now you're running out? It's Saturday, Beck —
BECKY. I need to find Steve — it sounds urgent —
JOE. How's the apartment working out?
BECKY. *(Starting offstage.)* Oh, it's fine — it's great —
JOE. Thought I'd come down and see you this week — spend the night —
BECKY. Oh, that's — that would be —
JOE. *(Overlapping.)* — maybe I'll sneak up, tap on your window — like we're back in your dorm room at the U.
BECKY. Just call first, okay? *(Becky is trying to leave, but Joe is holding her, playfully — )*
JOE. No way! I'm gonna surprise you! Doesn't that sound like FUN? *( — But now Becky pulls away, still trying to appease him — )*
BECKY. SO MUCH FUN. *(And lights instantly reveal: The Terrace. Morning. Walter has a tray with orange juice, coffee, newspaper, etc. Note: The light changes and opening lines of the following scenes should be IMMEDIATE — forcing Becky to rush to keep up with the play. She rarely succeeds; the scenes often start without her.)*
WALTER. Later I thought we'd go into the city. Meet Kenni for lunch.
BECKY. But the drive, Walter —
WALTER. I'll have Rex bring the 'copter round. Kenni wants us

to meet her new boyfriend.

BECKY. Oh, sure, that would be — *(Becky's cell phone rings — LOUD. She tries to ignore it.)*

WALTER. I thought maybe the four of us could do something this weekend. Why is it I never see you on the weekends? *(Over sound of phone.)* Wouldn't something on the weekend be FUN?

BECKY. SO MUCH FUN. *(Into phone.)* Hello? — *(Living Room. Night. Into phone, same call.)* Oh, Mrs. Tipton — yes, I know you're still waiting for your car. The thing is — *(Joe walks through the room, brushing his teeth.)*

JOE. Comin' to bed?

BECKY. *(To Joe.)* Yes, just a — *(Quickly, on phone.)* No, I don't have that information with me — I would need to swing by my old office — *(Becky's Cubicle. Day. Into phone, same call.)* Okay, here we are: *(Re: info on her computer.)* It looks like they're giving us a new delivery estimate — just another day or so. You can wait another few days, can't you? *(No response.)* Are you there?! Mrs. Tipton?! *(Steve arrives — and hands Becky a business card.)*

STEVE. Say hello to the new assistant regional sales director!

BECKY. Steve, *you promised!* — You swore you would not talk to Buckley about —

STEVE. Turns out I was right! — Buckley *was* having an affair. Some hot little pharmacist who works nights as a stripper. I got my promotion and the wilderness co-op got a *huge* donation.

BECKY. That's amazing.

STEVE. Blackmail is fun! And I'm sorry, Becky — I don't know what I was thinking: You could never pull off an *affair!* — You don't *have it in you!* — Now, c'mon — let's celebrate —

BECKY. Steve, I've got to tell you something —

STEVE. — I've got some vegan cupcakes in the car. *(Living Room.)*

CHRIS. You'll meet her soon, I promise. Now, listen — *(Becky is digging through her purse.)*

BECKY. Does she have a name, Chris? Can you tell me that much at least?!

CHRIS. *(Re: her digging.) Mom, what the hell are you doing?*

BECKY. I'm trying to find my LIPSTICK.

CHRIS. And I'm trying to TALK TO YOU. There's a new *vibe* in the house and I thought we should rap about it.

BECKY. "Rap about it?!"

CHRIS. I don't know how down you are with reciprocal determinism — but there are certain emerging factors in our home that begin to pose a definitive question.
BECKY. Like what?
CHRIS. Do you think Dad's cheating on you? *(Off her look.)* Little things. He doesn't answer his cell anymore. Won't say where he's going at night. I'm sure you've noticed.
BECKY. Um …
CHRIS. How are things in the … romantic quadrant?
BECKY. The *what?*
CHRIS. Any problem there? *(The Terrace. Day. Joe enters, in work garb, with a clipboard — followed by Kenni.)*
JOE. Nothing that can't be fixed.
KENNI. Thanks for coming all the way out here.
JOE. No problem.
KENNI. Now, I'll need to say good night — we're having guests for dinner.
JOE. Great old house. *(He hands a piece of paper to Kenni.)* Here's the estimate for the roof. Any questions, just give a call. *(Joe exits, just as — the Terrace. Night. — Ginger enters, opposite.)*
GINGER. Kenni, your dad's looking for you.
KENNI. Okay, thanks. *(And Kenni goes.)*
GINGER. Rebecca — *(Becky appears, holding a flute of champagne.)*
BECKY. Yes?
GINGER. — You look right at home. *(Becky points into the distance.)*
BECKY. Walter tells me that's your house.
GINGER. It was. Belongs to the bank now.
BECKY. So, where are you staying?
GINGER. I'm at the Holiday Inn — near the ferry terminal.
BECKY. You're *living there?*
GINGER. And working weekends as a hostess. The money's no good, but they're training me to bartend.
BECKY. Ginger —
GINGER. You taught me this, Rebecca. That a woman can turn the page. *(Walter and Kenni enter.)*
WALTER. Hello, ladies. Our guests have arrived — and you'll never guess who's here?
BECKY. Who?
WALTER. Bill Buckley! He's used my billboards for years — and without his cars I would have never met you.

GINGER. Isn't that sweet?
BECKY. Um …
WALTER. His wife is out of town, so he brought his niece. Her name is Amber. She's a pharmacist.
KENNI. And my new boyfriend is here, too —
BECKY. I wonder if —
KENNI. *(Gesturing offstage.)* — I really want you to meet him!
BECKY. — if you'd excuse me for a minute. *(And Becky leaves in a rush, as — a light on Walter.)*
WALTER. *(On his phone.)* Was it me? Was I out of line? *(Becky's Car. Night.)*
BECKY. *(On her phone.)* — No — no, Walter, it's okay — I just —
WALTER. The way you ran out of here — didn't even greet the guests —
BECKY. Yes, I know — *but it was just TOO MUCH tonight, Walter* — and if I miss the last ferry — *(Living Room. Night. Steve sits in the darkened room. He is eating chips.)*
STEVE. Becky, is that you?
BECKY. *Steve?*
STEVE. What time is it? *(She turns on a light. Sees him.)*
BECKY. It's after midnight …
STEVE. I hoped someone might be here. But Chris had a dinner party — and Joe's driving back from Cedar Cove.
BECKY. He's *what?*
STEVE. He was bidding a job out there.
BECKY. I didn't know that.
STEVE. *Isn't it amazing the things we don't know?* Like Buckley selling the company. What are we gonna do now?!
BECKY. Buckley did *what?*
STEVE. I heard those of us who just got promoted are gonna be the first to go! *(Becky's cell phone rings. A light on Walter.)*
WALTER. *(On his phone.)* You'll never guess where I am? Right here in the city — and I'm gonna swing by! *(Becky's Car.)*
BECKY. *(On her phone.)* I'm not home, Walter. I'm driving. *(A light on Joe. Walter remains lit.)*
JOE. *(On his cell.)* Hey, Beck — I'm ten minutes away.
BECKY. You're *what?*
WALTER. Meet me for a pizza. There's a place called Angelo's.
BECKY. Oh, Walter, I —
JOE. I was bidding a job down here — thought I'd swing by the

Mega-'Ship.
BECKY. Oh, Joe, I'm —
JOE. And hey, I stopped by the apartment. Doesn't look like you were ever there.
BECKY. Listen to me —
JOE. See you in a few! WALTER. Meet you there!
*(Joe and Walter both remain lit, as Becky continues to drive. Becky's Car. Late night.)*
BECKY. What I really want to do is keep driving ... NOT to see Walter — NOT home to my family — I'd rather just ... *drive away ... in some other car ... any car other than this one ... (The lights on Joe and Walter expand around them, until we realize they are standing in the Living Room. Day. The two men stare at each other. They set their cell phones down.)*
JOE. Want another beer?
WALTER. Sure. *(Joe gets him one.)* That was really good pizza.
JOE. Angelo's is not bad.
WALTER. And they bring it to your house. I love that.
JOE. They don't do that where you live?
WALTER. Not unless I send the 'copter.
JOE. God, could I do some roofing with a helicopter.
WALTER. I'm told I need some roofing. At my house. Up on the roof.
JOE. Who told you that.
WALTER. Kenni had a man out.
JOE. So, you've got a leak somewhere? *(Points to trash can.)* Like that one.
WALTER. Yes, I do. And you *put a bucket under it.* What a good idea.
JOE. What did you do?
WALTER. I'd rather not say. *(They drink their beers.)* Must be hard work — roofing. Keeping people dry.
JOE. Pays the bills. And I get to stand on people's houses.
WALTER. I would like that. But not the heat. Not the weather. Not the noise — and all those tools. Not the *work* part of it. I'd complain. I'm pretty sure I'd complain. You probably don't complain.
JOE. I learned something a long time ago, Walter: No one — and I mean no one on earth — wants to hear how busy you are, how tired you are, or what happened to you at the airport. *(They drink their beers.)*

WALTER. Are you going to kill me, Joe?
JOE. I don't think so.
WALTER. That's wonderful. As I was driving over here — I started to think that maybe you were …
JOE. … Laying a trap?
WALTER. Yes.
JOE. An ambush.
WALTER. Something like that. *(Beat.)* Are you?
JOE. Did you think I'd just let it go?
WALTER. What I thought was … I thought you were dead.
JOE. I'm not dead.
WALTER. That much is clear. But Becky kept insisting you *were* — and so I didn't fear a living guy who might kill me. I feared, you know, a dead guy who might just … *haunt me for awhile.*
JOE. Oh, I can still haunt you, Walter. You can count on that. *(Pause. They drink.)*
WALTER. So … when did you know?
JOE. Little things. Becky's clothes started to smell like fresh pine. Red dirt on the tires of her car. Receipts to the ferry in the glove box.
WALTER. *(Impressed.)* Joe, you're a regular dick.
JOE. I'm gonna let that one go, Walter.
WALTER. And what now? How do you plan to tell her?
JOE. I don't. *(Off Walter's look.)* She has her secret. Now, I have mine.
WALTER. You can't be —
JOE. You owe me this much, at least. I want to see what happens next. How she plans to keep pulling this off.
WALTER. But what about the kids?
JOE. Nothing. We're not gonna say a word to them. Got me? *(Chris enters, joyous — wearing a sport coat and loose tie. Carries an open bottle of champagne. He does not immediately see Walter.)*
CHRIS. Dad — where's Mom? — I need Mom to hear this too!
JOE. She'll be back soon.
CHRIS. But we can't wait! We're on our way to buy something — something *very important* — Kenni's in the car and — *(Chris now turns and sees Walter. Baffled.)* And her dad is in our living room…?
WALTER. Hello, Chris. That's a sporty blazer.
CHRIS. Mr. Flood —why are you —

JOE. Walter, where do you know my son from?
CHRIS. That's what's so weird and awesome — see, the girl I've been wanting you to meet —
JOE. Kenni, right?
CHRIS. — Right, well she's — I mean, Mister Flood is her — *(Kenni enters.)*
KENNI. Dad? What are you doing here?
CHRIS. *(To Kenni.)* They know each other! Isn't that awesome?
JOE. You mean to tell me …
CHRIS. *(Re: Kenni.)* This is her, Dad. *(Re: Walter.)* And this is her dad.
JOE. I know Kenni.
CHRIS. You what? WALTER. How's that?
JOE. *(To Kenni.)* I stood on your house.
CHRIS. That's amazing! KENNI. Oh, right —
KENNI. *(Re: Walter.)* — But how do you know —
JOE. We have someone in common, right, Walter?
WALTER. *(Re: champagne bottle.)* Is that empty?
CHRIS. Let me get you a glass — *(But Walter has already grabbed the bottle — taken a big swig from it.)*
JOE. So, what's the big news?
CHRIS. We really can't tell you till Mom gets here —
KENNI. — But we're on our way to buy a ring!
WALTER. Say again?
KENNI. We're gonna be married, Daddy. Isn't that amazing? *(Joe smiles and says:)*
JOE. Yes, it is! *(As Walter has more champagne.)*
KENNI. *(To Walter.)* I can't wait to tell Rebecca!
JOE. Oh, is that your Dad's new lady friend? We were just talkin' about her.
KENNI. She's great. I'll definitely want her at the wedding.
JOE. Oh, she'll be there.
CHRIS. You can't say a word to Mom. You've got to let us tell her.
JOE. I wouldn't miss that for the world.
KENNI. *(To Chris.)* What time's our appointment? CHRIS. *(To Kenni.)* We should be going.
JOE. Perfect. *(And Kenni and Chris are gone.)* Another beer, Walter?
WALTER. You have anything stronger?
JOE. Like what?
WALTER. Maybe a pistol.

JOE. Oh, cheer up: It's all gonna work out. Won't take long. Things unravel a lot more quickly than they, you know …
WALTER. … *Ravel?*
JOE. Exactly. Now, c'mon: Let's give her another call.
WALTER. I don't know, Joe —
JOE. You owe me this, Walter. And this time, a little *twist. (Joe is looking at their two cell phones, sitting side by side.)* Your phone. *(Lifts it.)* My phone. *(Lifts it.)* Oops. *(Joe purposefully switches the phones — giving his to Walter and keeping Walter's for his own.)*
WALTER. You can't be serious.
JOE. Press three for speed dial. Here we go … *(The men dial the phones — and stand near one another, waiting … )*
WALTER. So — just to be clear: Am I *you,* or *me?*
JOE. Up to you. But for god's sakes, Walter: *Have a little fun with it. (Listens.)* Voicemail.
WALTER. *(Starts to hang up.)* Oh, well.
JOE. *Leave a message.*
WALTER. But, Joe —
JOE. Don't make me *haunt you,* Walter. *(With a slight imitation of each other's voices, the men begin to leave their messages.)* Rebecca, it's me — Walter, your lover.
WALTER. Hello … this is Big Joe. Your hubby.
JOE. Oh, how my sailboat misses you.
WALTER. I just finished doing some roofing …
JOE. Darling, I've made some plans for us:
WALTER. … With my tools, up on some, you know, *roofs.*
JOE. I thought we'd climb in the 'copter and visit a few *graves. (Becky enters and stands in the room, unseen, behind the men. As she listens, she is frozen. She hears everything.)*
WALTER. And now I'm home here …
JOE. I'd like you to show me where they buried Joe.
WALTER. … Here at our home.
JOE. I'd love to pay my respects to the Old Dead Roofer. Wouldn't that be *keen?*
WALTER. *(To Joe, overhearing him.)* What in the world are you — *(And now, still unseen by the men, Becky quietly backs out of the room … and is gone.)*
JOE. And, hey, would you mind if I called you Becky? It has a nice ring to it.
WALTER. *(To Joe.)* I'm not doing this anymore …

JOE. And speaking of rings, *you'll never guess who Kenni is going to marry — (Stops short. A beat — they both listen.)* We got cut off. You did pretty good, Walter.
WALTER. Just kill me already. *(The Cubicle. Night.)*
BECKY. *(To audience.)* I didn't know where to go. So I came here. To my old job. Maybe I'd sleep under my desk. Maybe Walter Flood would walk in, like that very first night — *(A quick light on Walter.)*
WALTER. Good evening.
BECKY. *(Shouts.) I'M MARRIED AND MY HUSBAND IS ALIVE!!!*
WALTER. Good-bye. *(Walter is gone.)*
BECKY. — And I would realize that it had all been a dream. *(She sees something out the window.)* And that's when I saw it. It must have been delivered after-hours. It was at the edge of the lot, gleaming in the moonlight:

Mrs. Tipton's new car. Sleek and smart and fully loaded. And right next to it …

Another one. Identical. There's been some mistake … they've sent *two cars* … and that would explain the delay …

I checked our database for inventory and delivery. Mrs. Tipton's car was there, on the books — but as for the second car, *the identical car* … there was nothing. No one knew it was there. I called Mrs. Tipton. Told her the good news. She asked if she could get the car right away — *tonight.* I didn't see why not. She was on her way.

I finished the paperwork on Mrs. Tipton's car. Then I grabbed our universal key and put it in my purse — and I walked out into the night to see that second car … *(Becky's NEW Car. Late night.)* … it was luminous. I got inside. It enveloped me like a cult.

I wrote down the VIN number of this second car, this phantom vehicle. I walked back inside — went into the database — entered this VIN number — and this time the name of the registered owner came up: *Becky Foster.* It was my bonus from Buckley. If I never got my new life … at least I had my new car. *(The silhouette of Mrs. Tipton is seen, as before … )*

Mrs. Tipton arrived. When she saw her car, she said, "May I go? May I finally just *go?*" I said sure. I walked back inside to get her final paperwork, her warranty and extra key …

… And that's when I heard it. I heard that car's engine roar to life. And I raced to the door and called across the lot — telling her to wait just one more minute — *(The silhouette fades away.)* But she was gone. And her car was still there. She had taken the wrong car. She had driven away in *mine. With my purse on the seat next to her.*

Instinct took over. I jumped in *her* car — fired it up — oh, man, the sound of that thing, like the roar of a velvet tiger — and now I was chasing her towards the freeway. I made the exit ramp not long after she did — and I had that black car in my sights — a shadow chasing its shadow — but that woman — I should have known — she had nothing to lose — there was no catching her, hard as I tried … and ten miles out of town, I lost her for good … … *but I kept driving* — leaving the lights of the city in my wake. Every billboard I passed had the same two words at the bottom: Walter Flood, Walter Flood, Walter Flood, mile after mile. My reasons for going back were as strong as ever … but they were not as strong as this car … this thing moving through the night … putting miles between me and my life.

Two days later, in a motel room six hundred miles away from home … I turned on a television, and I learned what happened to Mrs. Tipton: *(Becky speaks from the car, as … the room around her gradually fills with people carrying devotional candles: Joe, Walter, Chris, Kenni, Steve and Ginger. The men wear dark suits; the women are in black. They set the candles around the room.)* She had driven all the way to Deception Pass — to the bridge that spans those rugged waters — and when she reached that bridge in the middle of the night, she floored it — and she was gone … safely over that bridge and straight ahead to that first sharp turn overlooking the sea — where apparently she floored it again … *and she did not turn* — and the guardrail did not stop her — and that amazing machine continued to roar as it soared through the air — and fell — a sheer drop — down into the night … into the churning waters below.

Her body was not found. The divers worked for several days … but found only the car, registered in *my name.*

And a purse, which contained several forms of identification, *all mine.*

The driver was presumed to be dead.

And to be me. *(Living Room. Evening. The mood is somber. Chris and Kenni are serving mugs of coffee. A moment between them:)*
KENNI. I can't believe we're doing this. So soon.

CHRIS. It's what Dad wanted.
KENNI. You okay? *(Chris says nothing and moves away. Ginger and Joe:)*
GINGER. I'm Ginger. A friend of Walter's. Rebecca — *Becky* — was just the — *(Stops.)*
JOE. Yes?
GINGER. I was going to say she was the best thing that ever happened to Walter. I'm sorry.
JOE. No — I understand. Thanks for being here. *(Steve approaches them.)* Do you know our friend Steve?
GINGER. Hello. STEVE. Hi, there.
JOE. Steve worked with Becky. At the dealership.
STEVE. *(To Joe.)* How you holdin' up, Joe?
JOE. *(Not good.)* Oh, you know … you've been there …
STEVE. Yes, I have. *(Joe moves away, leaving Ginger and Steve.)* We had candles at Rita's memorial, too.
GINGER. Everyone has candles, Steve. *(Beat.)* You sell cars?
STEVE. I'm afraid I do. Or used to. Before it all, you know … crumbled into dust. And your line of work is what?
GINGER. Pardon?
STEVE. Oh god, I'm sorry — it's just small talk, I know — but I'm not really good at it — I'm not good at making my talk *small enough* when I talk to people who are … *female* … *people.* I'm way out of practice.
GINGER. Steve.
STEVE. Yes?
GINGER. I would very much like you to ask what I do for a living.
STEVE. Okay, well —
GINGER. I bartend.
STEVE. Really?
GINGER. Yes. Five nights and Saturday lunch.
STEVE. I see.
GINGER. I'm pretty good at it. *(Beat. He stares at her.)*
STEVE. I was just headed to the kitchen.
GINGER. Were you now?
STEVE. I brought some pomegranate spritzer.
GINGER. I brought some scotch. *(Ginger goes toward the kitchen … and Steve follows her. Walter and Joe:)*
WALTER. It didn't have to end like this, Joe.
JOE. Maybe not.

WALTER. I'll never understand it — you wanted to see how far she'd push it —
JOE. Right.
WALTER. — How far she'd go to pull it off?
JOE. And now we know. *(Walter moves away, lost, as — Kenni joins them.)*
KENNI. I'm sorry, Mr. Foster.
JOE. Keep an eye on your old man, okay? — He's taking this hard. *(Chris joins them.)*
CHRIS. You need anything, Dad?
JOE. We should head to the restaurant. They're holding a room for us. Will you tell the others?
CHRIS. Sure.
JOE. *(More intimate.)* She's okay, Chris. She's in a better place. You gotta believe that. *(Chris nods — and then circulates amid the others, as — everyone finishes their coffees, grabs their jackets, purses, etc. … and leaves. The last person remaining in the room is Joe. Joe places the eight-by-ten photo of himself and Becky in a prominent place … sets a few candles in front of it … and then, as he starts to leave: Becky appears, opposite, behind him. She wears a long coat.)*
BECKY. *(Quietly.)* It's nice. *(Joe turns, sees her.)* You imagine it, I guess. What your family, your friends — what they'll do when you're gone. *(Silence.)* Joe…? Please say something … *(In silence, he walks to her, stands before her. We await the embrace, but instead he simply says:)*
JOE. You hungry? *(He moves away — taking off his suit coat, loosening his tie.)*
BECKY. Joe…?
JOE. I think we've got some cold cuts.
BECKY. I missed you, Joe.
JOE. Mm-hmm.
BECKY. And I'm sorry — I'm so sorry — but I just had to —
JOE. So, how was being dead? Around here, it didn't go over so great.
BECKY. Yes — I know — but please let me tell you this: *(He pops open a beer. Finally gestures: Go ahead.)* I drove … and I lost track of time. Avoided the news — didn't read a paper — just found a road and followed it. It was so strange. I knew what people thought happened. Knew no one was looking for me. That I could turn that car in any direction I wanted. I could go anywhere.

JOE. They found the body.
BECKY. What?
JOE. Beverly Tipton. Her body washed up. A few days ago. The state patrol called me. Told me you were no longer presumed dead. Only missing. *(She stares at him … stares at the room, the candles … )*
BECKY. But if you *knew — why would you do all this if —*
JOE. I didn't tell them. Any of them.
BECKY. You let them think I was dead?
JOE. No. I think you did that. *(Beat.)* Look, Beck — there are things you want me to say, and God knows someday I'll probably say 'em, but not yet. Right now I've just got to live with it a little. And so do you.
BECKY. But I just wanted to —
JOE. *(Sharp.) You don't get to put a marker in your life.* Oh, you can walk away, you can always walk away — but you don't get to come back to the same place you left. Ask anyone. *(Indicates an audience member.)* Ask this guy. Am I right?

*(To the audience member, as needed.)* (See, I told you.) // (I'll talk to you later.)

*(To the same audience member.)* Did she offer you a beer? *(Gets response.)* You want one?

*(As needed.)* (Okay, here you go.) // (If you change your mind, the fridge is right there.) *(If the audience member says yes to the beer, Joe gets him one.)*

BECKY. What are you doing?
JOE. What's it look like? You think I can't see *these people?*
BECKY. Joe, listen —
JOE. No, you listen to me — I'm gonna tell you how this goes: *(Joe gestures to the booth and immediately lights isolate Joe. Turns to audience.)* I called Chris at the restaurant. Told him that his mom was home, and safe. And everyone came back to the house. *(The Living Room. Night. The candles remain lit. Chris, Walter, Kenni, Steve and Ginger appear at the edges of the room, surrounding: Becky. Long silence. Finally … )*
KENNI. *(Quietly.)* Welcome home.
BECKY. Thank you. *(Kenni embraces Becky. Then she turns to the others … )*
KENNI. Chris? … Dad? … *(Chris and Walter do not move. Instead: Steve steps forward.)*

STEVE. It was terrible, Becky.
BECKY. Yes, I'm —
STEVE. It was like being on that mountain again. When Chris first called me —
KENNI. He had heard from my Dad.
WALTER. It was Ginger who saw it.
GINGER. Saw it on the news.
STEVE. We all rushed over here —
KENNI. We were glued to the TV —
WALTER. Making calls —
GINGER. Trying to find you, Rebecca —
STEVE. Trying to imagine where you'd gone. *(Beat.)* Where had you gone?
CHRIS. *(Sharp, angered.)* It's called paranormal transference. When the soul tires of its "host body" and seeks a new identity, a new vessel to inhabit.
BECKY. No, Chris — really, that's not what I was —
CHRIS. *(Points to Kenni.)* THAT WAS MY GIRLFRIEND, MOM. That's who you've wanted to meet — but you already know her, since you've been shacked up with her old man!
BECKY. I'm sorry — JOE. Chris, please —
CHRIS. But, the thing is: She's not my girlfriend anymore —
BECKY. Oh, no, that's —
CHRIS. — SHE'S MY FIANCÉE ... How *weird and awesome is that, HUH, MOM?!*
BECKY. Chris, if you'd listen — if ALL of you, please, could just let me say this: *(A charged beat. They are all staring at her, listening.)* When it started, I didn't know what to make of it. And I didn't know why. But now — looking back on it — it's so clear to me —
CHRIS. That's "hindsight bias."
STEVE. Very common.
CHRIS. Once an outcome is known, we tend to think we could have foreseen it, somehow. It's total arrogance!
WALTER. And total *hogwash.*
STEVE. I agree. JOE. Amen to that.
GINGER. *(Sharp, to the men.)* Are you boys *finished?! (To Becky.)* Becky, — I, for one, am glad you're home.
STEVE. We're all *glad,* Ginger, but the point is —
GINGER. That's not what it sounds like.
STEVE. *(Suddenly.)* I was going to ask you to go hiking!

GINGER. I don't *hike,* Steve.
STEVE. I knew you'd say that! I knew you weren't Rita. That you could *never* be Rita. That I can *never* go on that hike again. That it's *over. (Silence. Steve turns to Becky.)* It's over, isn't it? *(Becky looks at him … and nods.)* What do we do now? *(Becky has no answer. Steve just stands there, lost. Then …)*
GINGER. *(To Steve.)* You ever worn a pair of nice Italian loafers? Hand-molded leather, artisan-cured.
STEVE. No — but please keep talking.
GINGER. Get your coat. *(Ginger nods, cordially, to the others and is out the door. Steve starts to follow, but then stops, looks back into the room.)*
STEVE. Becky, I want you to know —
JOE. Steve: GO. *(Steve nods and goes, quickly. Chris approaches Walter.)*
CHRIS. I'm sorry, Mr. Flood — I wanted to do this right.
WALTER. You think you can outsmart it, don't you?
CHRIS. Sir?
WALTER. Look at you! Love has made you so impossibly stupid. I bet songs on the radio make you cry. You probably have a favorite booth at your restaurant and a dessert you love to share. You still call each other in the middle of the day for no reason at all — *(To the others.) Look at them!* They're so fearless. It's *breathtaking. (To Kenni and Chris.)* You really believe it, don't you? You think you'll *be the First Two People in History to beat love to the punch* — to *get it before it gets you.*
CHRIS. Yes, sir. We do.
WALTER. Well, then, Chris and Kenni … as your elder … it is my responsibility … to let you *go on believing the impossible* — to not tell you otherwise. *Go do it.* Go kick love's ass — and when you're done, give it an extra kick in the ribs for me. *(Walter takes Kenni's hand.)* Of course I'll be at the wedding. Just don't make me shop for a gift.
CHRIS. Thank you, sir. *(To Kenni.)* The ring is ready. The jeweler is open till nine — we can still get there.
KENNI. It's okay … we can wait a little.
CHRIS. All right — tomorrow's good, too —
KENNI. There's nothing wrong —
CHRIS. Sure, whenever —
KENNI. — With waiting a little … giving it a little time. *(She has stepped away from him. Gently.)* I'd like that … I'd like to …

just step back a little … okay? *(Chris just stares at her. To Becky.)* And someday … I'd like to talk to you. *(And Kenni goes. Silence.)*
WALTER. Give her all the time she needs, Chris. And when she's ready … *(Walter reaches into a pocket and removes a small velvet box.)* Perhaps you'll give her this. *(Walter hands the small box to Chris. Walter nods — and Chris opens the box … revealing a stunning diamond ring.)*
CHRIS. Mr. Flood…?
WALTER. It was meant to be in the family … *(A look at Becky.)* Just in a different way. *(Walter extends his hand … Chris shakes it — and leaves. An awkward silence.)*
JOE. Well. Just us three. Should I get a deck of cards?
BECKY. Joe …
JOE. Walter's starting to feel right at home here.
WALTER. Another beer, Joe?
JOE. Sure, Walt. *(To Becky, re: Walter.)* We've had some real good chats.
WALTER. *(Getting the beer.)* And Joe didn't kill me.
JOE. That option is nearly completely off the table.
BECKY. There's no way I can explain — to either of you — all the things I learned about —
JOE. *(Sharp.)* You're right — you can't. Because *we don't want to know. (Walter brings Joe a beer.)* Thanks, Walt. And this is where we say good-bye. You have my card. Call me about your roof.
WALTER. *(Caught off guard.)* Yes, sure, all right … *(Walter is looking at Becky, as — Joe speaks to the audience.)*
JOE. And as I stood there with my wife: I watched Walter Flood give Rebecca a final look … and then he walked out of our home and — *(Walter starts offstage.)*
BECKY. Wait a minute. *(Walter stops. To Joe.)* What are you doing?
JOE. Just telling them what happened.
BECKY. You're not going to let me say good-bye to him?
JOE. Wasn't planning on it.
BECKY. *Just a word or two?!*
JOE. *(Beat.)* Okay. *(To audience.)* And then — as Walter turned to leave — Becky said to him:
BECKY. Walter, I want you to know —
JOE. *But it was too late.* He was gone. Out the door and into the night. *(Walter leaves.)* She never saw him again. *(To Becky.)* Or did you?

BECKY. No. *(Now: Becky moves around the room, turning off the lamps and lights; [perhaps] blowing out the candles.)*
JOE. *(To audience.)* Becky got her old job back. She lost the raise and promotion, of course — but they offered to let her keep the car.
BECKY. Joe, we don't need that car — there might be too many bad memories, you know?
JOE. To which I said: Are you crazy? *Of course we're keeping the car!* — And that was that. Life went on. Becky thought about maybe going back to school. Massage therapy.
BECKY. Joe?
JOE. Hmm?
BECKY. Not now … but sometime, someday … could you ever …
JOE. Forgive and forget? *(She nods.)* Probably not. *(Pause. She nods.)* But, it'll be okay, Beck.
*BECKY.* Why? How?
JOE. I'm a roofer. I'll cover it. Just cover it over. *(Music, as Becky turns off the final light in the room … To audience.)* We started taking long drives together in that car. *(And we are once again back in Becky's New Car. Sunset. Becky sits. Joe pulls up a chair next to her. He is driving.)* One day we even took that car up to Cedar Cove. From the road we saw divers trolling the waters, near Walter's dock. They were searching for a wedding ring. Other days, we just …
BECKY. … Drove.
JOE. Radio on.
BECKY. Together.
JOE. Traffic moving, nice and easy. *(Pause.)*
BECKY. *(Staring front, simply.)* Heaven. *(Music builds and plays out, as — lights fade to black.)*

**End of Play**

## PROPERTY LIST

Rubber cleaning glove
Toilet plunger
New roll of toilet paper
Dustbuster
Cleaning rag
Empty trash can
Newspaper section
Magazines
Nearly empty carton of Diet Sprite
Office phone
Pencil
Textbook
Pizza box
Paperwork
4 cell phones
Sports section
Notebook
Stapler
Brochure
Calculator with paper tape
Wedding rings
3 business cards
Watch
Throw pillow
Mugs of coffee
Printout of driving route
Flier
Stack of invoices
Framed 8x10 photo of Becky and Joe
Coat, dress, shoes, makeup and hair stuff
Jewelry
Key
Bottle of water
Purse with lipstick and car keys
Cocktails
Martini
Bag of chips
Glass of wine

Reading glasses
Bills
2 cups of coffee
Crutches
Towel
Hairbrush
Tray with orange juice, coffee, newspaper
Toothbrush
Computer
Clipboard with piece of paper
Flute of champagne
Beers
Bottle of champagne
Devotional candles
Ring box with diamond ring

## SOUND EFFECTS

Vacuum cleaner
Things falling and crashing
Phone rings
Car horn honks
Cell phone rings
Cocktail party music

## NOTES

*(Use this space to make notes for your production)*

## NOTES

*(Use this space to make notes for your production)*

## NOTES

*(Use this space to make notes for your production)*

# NOTES

*(Use this space to make notes for your production)*

# NOTES

*(Use this space to make notes for your production)*

## NOTES

*(Use this space to make notes for your production)*

## NOTES

*(Use this space to make notes for your production)*